CAMBRIDGE
STUDENT
PRANKS

CAMBRIDGE STUDENT PRANKS

A History of Mischief & Mayhem

JAMIE COLLINSON

The History Press

Frontispiece: King's College Chapel. (Linda Hall)

First published 2010

The History Press
The Mill, Brimscombe Port
Stroud, Gloucestershire, GL5 2QG
www.thehistorypress.co.uk

British Library Cataloguing in Publication Data.
A catalogue record for this book is available from the British Library.

ISBN 978 0 7524 5395 8

Typesetting and origination by The History Press
Printed in Great Britain

CONTENTS

INTRODUCTION

I will never forget my first experience of Cambridge – chiefly because for most of it I was lost and mildly terrified. I had come to visit Sidney Sussex College before my interview. Having missed the official open day, the college had kindly allowed me to visit and arranged a meeting with the admissions tutor. I always felt that I received special attention due to my privileged education at a state school. (At the time the University was particularly keen to show that it displayed no favouritism to public schools and I'm sure this worked in my favour.)

I had arrived by train and with youthful high spirits decided to walk into town to get a better picture of the city which I hoped to make my home for the next three years. I would later learn that the city had placed the railway station so far from the centre to make it difficult for students to visit their boyfriends or girlfriends in London. As a result, I had a tedious, long walk in an uncomfortable suit.

Having grown up in a Victorian town I was used to decidedly longer, wider and less winding streets. Later I would look after American summer school students who would often remark with wonder, 'It's as if they were built with no thought to cars isn't it?' Although I now think them charming and beautiful, I remember vividly my confusion at the time. Before long I was confronted with the University Library. Can there be a more intimidating structure to new and hopeful students? An industrial-looking building, it shares the architect with and bears a striking resemblance to the Tate Modern in London. The immense, dark tower has always made me think of Ozymandias – 'Look on my works, ye mighty, and despair'.

In spite of this inauspicious start, I made it to my meeting, which went well, and after an interview was offered a place. I soon fell in love with the city; it is a magical place. Among the narrow streets and ancient buildings are hidden halls and homes in which lived some of the finest minds in history. Their essence seems to permeate the place and can be a source of inspiration or fear of inadequacy to visitors. Along with that air of genius is the whiff of mischief. Thousands of great young minds, cooped up together, have produced some of the best practical jokes and hoaxes the world has ever seen. Pranks have varied from the frivolous acts of privileged youth to worthy political statement. For every drunken midnight escapade or case of an obnoxious young aristocrat knocking a policeman's hat off, there has been a clever and unique joke which has delighted the public.

I must warn the reader that some of the tales in this book may be apocryphal. Parts of it are based on stories passed down from student to student. Academics, like everyone else, enjoy embellishing a good tale and their memories cannot be wholly trusted. I will, however, do my best to indicate what I think dubious. None of this, though, diminishes the ingenuity of the stories. If this has an aim it is to highlight the playfulness of intelligence and the fertile garden it finds in Cambridge.

Here's to the pranksters, hackers, jokers and phreakers. The cleverest stunts have often come from the cleverest people, and they should be celebrated.

Jamie Collinson, 2010

ONE

WELCOME TO COLLEGE LIFE

INTERVIEWS

I'm afraid that I must start this book with bad news for prospective Cambridge (or Oxford) students. It's not only students who enjoy a prank, and for Cambridge dons a good source of fun is the round of interviews each winter. Though not pranks *per se*, it is instructive to take a short look at the admissions process, as it will shed light on the spirit of playfulness evident in the University. Though at times stuffy and old-fashioned (a well-known college joke goes, 'How many dons does it take to change a lightbulb?' and is answered in an incredulous tone, 'Change?'), as a whole the institution is happy to take a joke in good humour, and at times play one too.

Though they'll earnestly tell you that the interview process is 'necessarily rigorous to select the very best from the enormous pool of talented individuals who apply, particularly in light of ever increasing A Level results,' I think we can all see how it might be fun to force candidates to 'think outside the box'. I'm not saying that the interviews are cruel (in fact my own experience would indicate quite the opposite), but there are many stories of unusual questions being set to test applicants. The most famous example is the logically torturous question to a would-be student of philosophy, 'Is this a question?' Incidentally, the brave applicant of the story answers, 'Is this an answer?' – exceptionally clever but I fear it is far too quick-witted to be a real response.

The rationale behind these questions is simple. By asking questions which require lateral thinking the candidate can be assessed on how they think, rather than how well they've been coached for the interview. Here are a few of my favourite recorded questions:

Q. What is the future of the British coal industry? (Answer: smoke)
Q. Can you write a formula that proves mathematics is interesting?
Q. Would you rather be a novel or a poem?
Q. What would you do if you were a magpie?
Q. How would you poison someone without the police finding out?

EXAMS

For most at Cambridge their student life is book-ended by interviews and exams. The University divides its bachelor's degrees by Tripos – an undergraduate student of mathematics is said to be reading for the Mathematical Tripos, while a student of chemistry (or any of the other sciences) reads for the Natural Sciences Tripos (and in the case of the chemist chooses courses specific to chemistry). Many mistakenly believe that the word relates to the usual three years of study, and thus their degree was studied in three ('tri') parts. In fact the etymology is much more mundane, tracing to the three-legged stool which candidates once sat on to take their exams. One apocryphal legend still very popular claims that students received one leg of the stool for each year of their study, resulting in a complete stool at the end of their degree.

The Tripos system is ancient, having evolved gradually with the University. Until the nineteenth century only one Tripos was available: the Mathematical Tripos, known formally as the 'Senate House Examination'. It has always been a difficult exam, and along with the interviews has historically been one of the few outlets for Cambridge dons to have a little fun at the expense of students.

By way of example, consider the 1854 Mathematical Tripos – sixteen papers spread over eight days, totalling 44.5 hours and 211 questions. The questions were extremely difficult and even the best would not have time to complete the exam. There is a record of one exam from the 1860s which had a total possible mark of 17,000. The student with the top first (the senior wrangler) managed 7, 634 (a little under 45 per cent), while the next best student scored 4,123 (24 per cent) and the lowest score was 237 (1.4 per cent). Things have got a little better since then as the excessively taxing questions have been discouraged. However, it can still be a shock to new students used to scoring above 90 per cent in A Level exams to be told that their mark of 40 per cent in the Mathematical Tripos has resulted in a first!

With this kind of mental bashing, it is little surprise that during exam term students, like men at war, acquire a certain graveyard humour. An example where students and dons conspired was the awarding of the infamous wooden spoon. Until reforms in 1910 the results of all those taking the Mathematical Tripos were listed in descending order of performance, divided into Wranglers (firsts), Senior Optimes (seconds) and Junior Optimes (thirds). Those who were left scored either an ordinary (a pass without honours) or a fail.

The wooden spoon was awarded to the student with the lowest mark to still receive honours – i.e. the person with the lowest third-class degree. The term 'wooden spoon' or 'the spoon' came to be applied to the recipient as well, and the prize became notorious and quite celebrated:

> And while he lives, he wields the boasted prize
> Whose value all can feel, the weak, the wise;
> Displays in triumph his distinguish'd boon,
> The solid honours of the Wooden Spoon.
> 'The Wooden Spoon' from *The Cambridge Tart* (1823)

Many have recounted that being 'the spoon' came to hold a certain kudos, particularly with students of a humorous disposition. Some went so far as to claim that students would retake exams to attempt a worse mark and gain the coveted spoon, though of course no-one wanted to score too low and receive an ordinary. The spoons are also well recorded in literature, with the first use in the 1803 *Gradus ad Cantabrigiam* – 'Wooden spoon for wooden heads: the lowest of the Junior Optimes'. In *Cambridge Memories* (1936) Thomas Thornley said of the spoon:

> If its recipient was a man of sense, he would seize upon it joyously, and, brandishing it over his head, march off with it as a valued trophy; but if, as sometimes happened, he was timid or nervous and shrank from it as a symbol of shame, it would, as like as not, pursue his retreating rear with sounding smacks.

Given these references, it is likely that the tradition dates back to at least the late eighteenth century, though it may be even older than that. As time passed the spoons themselves became larger and larger. Having originally been decorated wooden kitchen spoons, they became giant constructions, in later years, often being made of oars from rowing eights.

Exam results are read out from the upstairs balcony in Senate House to the students waiting anxiously below. A ceremony developed whereby the wooden spoon would be dangled from the balcony in front of the recipient. As he knelt before the Vice Chancellor two of his friends would each hold a piece of ribbon attached to the spoon and would solemnly walk towards each other, lowering the spoon in the process. Two other friends would cut the ribbon and present the spoon to the individual concerned. Clearly this could not take place without the consent of the establishment.

Unfortunately all good things come to an end, and in 1875 the University added a new statute banning 'the suspension of objects from the Senate House balcony' – this was widely seen as a change in the tolerance for the wooden spoon tradition. However, the giving of spoons continued in a more discreet fashion for another thirty-five years until 1910, when reforms to the Tripos system meant results were published in alphabetical rather than merit order, keeping the identity of the spoon secret.

The twilight years of the wooden spoon saw the most extravagant ever produced. In 1892 a student at Queens' College, Patrick Joseph O'Leary Bradbury, was awarded the spoon. It took the form of a 4ft malt shovel (used in the production of beer) decorated on one side with the arms of Queens' and on the other with the arms of the University. Thought to be the only spoon ever awarded to a Queensman, it is a proud possession of the family and a great reminder of their ancestor.

The last wooden spoon was awarded in 1909 to Cuthbert Lempriere Holthouse. In an act of grace, the University allowed this last spoon to be handed over at the graduation ceremony, though accounts differ on whether it was lowered from the balcony. An oarsman of the Lady Margaret Boat Club of St John's College, Holthouse's spoon was a magnificently modified oar. It was certainly over 5ft long, and from photographs of the time appears close to Holthouse's height, so could be up to 6ft. At the end of the handle was the large spoon bowl, which was decorated with the St John's crest and Holthouse's initials. The blade of the oar was inscribed with an epigram in Greek, translating as:

In Honours Mathematical
This is the very last of all
The Wooden Spoons which you see here
O you who see it, shed a tear.

Surviving wooden spoons are rare. This last spoon is in possession of St John's College with another kept at Selwyn College library. In 2009 St John's held an exhibition of five surviving examples, including the last, to mark the centenary of the awarding of the last wooden spoon.

Another example of exam-time humour is the oft repeated tale of 'Cake and Ales' (it's nothing to do with Somerset Maugham). This is a favourite for older students to tell their newer comrades-in-arms. It's an appealing story for anyone facing an examination, with just the right flavour of getting one up on the establishment. Unfortunately, as we shall see shortly, the tale is almost completely untrue.

The last wooden spoon. (Courtesy of Wikipedia)

We've all heard of those archaic un-repealed laws — like the one permitting the shooting of a Welshman with a crossbow after dark, or the other forbidding anyone firing a cannon close to a dwelling house (incidentally a similar law exists in Chico, California, where there is a fine of $500 for anyone detonating a nuclear device within the city limits). With these in mind, an enterprising student scours the University statutes and finds gold.

When it comes to his first exam he sits with the rest of the students, then, just as the exam is about to begin, he pipes up to proctor:

STUDENT: Before the exam starts please bring me cakes and ale.

PROCTOR: I beg your pardon?

STUDENT: Sir, I request that you bring me cakes and ale.

PROCTOR: Young man you must be out of your mind. I shall do no such thing.

STUDENT: Sir, I really must insist. I request and require that you bring me cakes and ale to act as sustenance during my examination.

At this point the student produces a copy of an ancient University statute, written in Latin but still nominally in force. He points to a section which translates roughly as 'Gentlemen sitting for the Tripos examinations may request and require cakes and ale.' After some discussion, the proctor and invigilator decide that they have no choice but to go along with the absurd request and offer scones and lemonade as a reasonable modern equivalent. The student accepts and happily enjoys his meal while completing his exam.

It is here that the story often differs. Students telling students will often leave it there. While academics, or anyone who has less time for youthful arrogance, will add that as he stood up to leave the exam hall the student was stopped by the proctor and promptly fined £5 for incorrect dress. When he asked what was wrong with his attire he was told that he failed to wear his sword to the examination and shown a similarly ancient piece of legislation.

A comparable tale exists along the lines that, due to the University's age, a statute exists for the provision of students leaving their studies to fight in the crusades. Under this provision, should an examinee arrive and claim that they cannot complete their exams as they are off to fight in the crusades, they shall be instantly granted a first-class degree for their patriotism. A student bravely attempted this trick with his proctor and was curtly told that he did not have the requisite white horse, sword or armour and should sit down and get on with his paper.

The variations on which item may be requested (e.g. a pint of beer, a glass of port, cakes and ale) and why the trickster loses out in the end (e.g. lack of sword, failure to arrive on a horse, not wearing shoes with silver buckles) all hint that the story may be more legend than fact. Sadly, although the story has been circulating since at least the 1950s, when it was written about in *The Lancet*, no such statute has ever been discovered. As the University is famous for keeping every minutiae of paperwork, it seems likely that the prank never occurred.

Pleasingly, the story seems to be the inspiration behind a little prank carried out by the great Peter Cook during his final examinations for the Modern and Medieval Languages Tripos. Cook did not enjoy the sweltering heat in the exam hall but was delighted to discover that he was entitled to bring a drink into the hall if he wished, though it was not common for students to do so. He first chose a carton of fruit juice to relieve his thirst, which, according to Harry Thompson's 1997 biography of Cook, annoyed the invigilating don who was 'himself sweating in full rig'. 'Peter kept up a running battle with this gentleman. The following day he openly swigged copious draughts from a bottle of brandy, informing the fuming official that he didn't want his answers to lack spirit.'

MATHEMATICIANS

On taking my place at Cambridge I joined the ranks of a peculiar species, the mathematician. While it was often remarked that I was 'quite normal, for a mathmo', others of my brethren were known for peculiar habits — not least the lecturers. One well-liked fellow would surreptitiously eat a piece of tissue paper at the end of his lectures, and was known for his surreal humour. On one memorable occasion he was filling in for a colleague. 'Some of the more observant of you will have realised that I am not Dr Beard,' he announced at the start of the lecture, 'but don't worry, tomorrow I will be.'

Two particular maths students were keen on a little fun during their supervisions. (These are tutorial sessions in which one or two students will spend time with a supervisor to go over the work set in lectures.) This particular pair (one male, one female) enjoyed seeing if they could get a raised eyebrow from the inscrutable Head of Mathematics. They began innocuously enough, wearing slightly odd clothes for their sessions, but before long were dressed in ball gown and black tie for each supervision. When the don continued to plough through their work on pure mathematics without a word about their attire, the male decided to step matters up a notch. Feeling amorous and mischievous he began to play a game of 'footsie' beneath the table, rubbing his foot against his partner's leg. His advances were reciprocated and for the rest of their supervision the pair continued their flirtatious game while the don droned on. Afterwards the male student exclaimed, 'I can't believe he didn't notice what was going on beneath the table!'

'What was going on?' replied the female mathematician. She had not been the one he was playing with, and they never joked during a supervision again.

MEDICS

Medical students are noted for the black humour they necessarily develop. Two stories come to mind, and though they were both told to me as tales from the Faculty of Medicine, I have been unable to find written accounts and think it quite likely that they have been travelling around various universities for years. The first is a simple tale of an unfortunate motorist. Passing through Cambridge, he encountered car trouble and stopped outside a University building. Unbeknownst to him, it is the building where dissections were practised, and when he popped inside and asked, 'will someone give me a hand?' he was horrified to be passed a cadaver's severed appendage.

The second is more famous, and as it was recently mentioned on the television show *House* we can assume it goes around the American universities too. A group of first year students are being given their introduction to anatomy. The instructor stands before a cadaver, with another body for each pair of students. 'It is very important that you become familiar with the human body and learn to follow instructions without being squeamish. Now, do as I do.' The instructor takes his finger and places it in the cadaver's rectum. The students reluctantly do the same. He then says, 'now the second step' and licks his finger. Wishing to impress, the students suppress revulsion and follow suit, with many gagging or throwing up. 'It is also very important to be observant,' the lecturer continues, 'for example, observe that I inserted my middle finger but licked my forefinger, whereas you all used the same finger for both.'

ROWING

At most colleges it is rare to find a student who has not sampled the pleasures of rowing. It is a sport held dear in Cambridge and the college boat clubs do their best to ensure that every freshman has a taste of it. One of the first social events held each term is a squash (party with free drinks) to recruit new oarsmen and women. Fresh-faced first years are plied with drink and regaled with tales of comradeship and glory in the May/Lent Bumps. Each inebriated young man (or woman) imagines the feeling of speeding along in a sleek eight with the morning sun on their back, and promptly signs up to join a novice boat. Before they know it, the harsh reality of learning to row in the winter hits them. There is nothing romantic about waking up for a 6 a.m. outing, getting soaking wet with freezing rain and then fighting to keep your eyes open during a 9 a.m. lecture. The blisters are not fun either. Many quickly back out of the boat club, but for some there is something heroic about the adversity and they carry on.

At the end of their first term, novices graduate to the senior boats. This is celebrated with a supper held by the boat club and is often a rowdy affair. I cannot speak for every college but at Sidney Sussex the novices were given challenges to complete to prove their devotion to the club. Typically they would involve streaking across courtyards and the theft of rival boat club mascots – short of that anything with another college's crest on it would do. At our novice dinner a friend struck upon the brilliant realisation that dressed in dinner jackets we all looked very much like waiters. Discovering that a dinner was being held at King's he entered the hall via a service entrance and calmly walked down the tables collecting stacks of crested crockery. He dined off formal dinnerware for the rest of his degree.

A well-known story at Sidney was that a previous novice challenge had seen a freshman head into St John's and remove a valuable portrait from the wall. The painting turned out to be alarmed and as soon as it was lifted a siren sounded. Panicking, the student didn't think to put down the painting and instead raced through the town back to Sidney and presented the painting to the boat club captain. The captain was impressed – until the police arrived to take back the £50,000 portrait. I have no evidence this ever happened but it was often spoken of amongst rowers. This is certainly no proof of veracity as it was also often said that when one of the paintings in hall was taken away for restoration the dirt on it had been analysed for historical interest and was found to be 80 per cent potato from food fights! Another was that during the challenges students had once painted a zebra crossing onto Sidney Street, connecting the college with Sainsbury's which sits opposite it. The crossing looked so realistic that for several weeks cars respected it, and grocery shopping was just that little bit easier.

Not all hijinks end so well. An infamous rowing legend tells of a prank gone badly wrong in 1876, when rowers at St John's College attached a ceremonial sword to the front of their boat, in order that they might sink the boat in front if they managed to bump it. The boat in front was one of Second Trinity's (at the time Trinity had three boat clubs – First open to all, Second for students of theology and Third for those who had been to Eton or Westminster) and was bumped by the John's boat. As the sword pierced the stern it hit and killed the cox. As a result, Second Trinity was dissolved in memoriam, leaving the First and Third Trinity Boat Club we have today. To punish St John's, their rowers were banned from using the college name, resulting in the Lady Margaret Boat Club. A wonderful legend, but not entirely true. A cox was killed by impaling during a bump but it was in 1888, involved Trinity Hall and Clare boats, and did not involve a sword. The front of a rowing eight proved quite sufficient to cause death on its own, and the incident led to the mandatory use of bow balls on the front of every college boat. Second Trinity was dissolved for the more prosaic reason that there were simply not enough theologians to recruit from.

These days rowers are well behaved (at least on the river) as the Cambridge University Combined Boat Club has quite strict regulations. The most you're likely to see at bumps is a crew throwing their cox into the water after the race.

PUNTING

There are no such regulations on punting. A trip along the backs on a hot summer day can seem like a cross between *Swallows and Amazons* and *Apocalypse Now*. Locals and students come out in droves for picnics, hapless tourists zig-zag along with little control of their boats and professional punt chauffeurs plough through the traffic in their twelve-seater ferry punts. If you plan to take a trip on the river, take my advice and avoid the post-lunch rush; a cruise in the morning or early evening is much more pleasant.

If you decide to punt the boat yourself then there are a few caveats to bear in mind. Firstly, watch out when you pass under bridges – not for the reason you're probably thinking. Any fool knows to duck so that he doesn't hit his head. Only experienced punters know to push extra hard as they enter the arch. Should you fail to do this and bring up your pole on the other side close to the parapet it is quite likely to be grabbed and stolen by a passing student. It is not a fun thing to be left adrift without your pole. Although you're likely to have the pole returned if you are on the Backs, the Grantchester stretch can be more dangerous. If you believe the local papers, the journey to Grantchester by river is strewn with feral children who will steal your punt pole and ransom it back to you.

Secondly, make sure you punt the Cambridge way, standing on the deck at the rear of the boat. Though it may be unusual elsewhere it is considered traditional in the city, and you are much more likely to fall foul of some joker if you don't comply. It is not clear how the practice came about. Robert Rivington's definitive *Punting: Its History and Techniques* suggests that standing on the deck was started by the female students at Girton wanting to cause a stir by showing off their ankles. A nice story which I hope is true.

Student boats are generally harmless, even if dressed as pirates and a little intoxicated. They're more of a danger to themselves than anyone else. Among their favourite punting activities is the old tradition of bridge climbing. This is sometimes done as a race in which two boats will set off from Jesus Green, the passengers on the boats must then climb up and over each bridge as it is passed. Between each bridge a pint of beer is traditionally consumed, and with nine bridges along the Backs it is certainly a challenging feat.

The most famous tale from the river must be the one regarding the Mathematical Bridge at Queens'. The legend goes that it was built by Isaac Newton and was cleverly constructed using state-of-the-art mathematics, thus requiring no nuts and bolts. Students took the bridge apart as a prank but were unable to put it back together again, and so it now has nuts and bolts aplenty. A lovely story but unfortunately not true at all. There was no prank, it was not built by Newton and there have always been nuts and bolts. It is a very pretty and impressive bridge though.

Lgend has it that the Mathematical Bridge initially required no nuts and bolts – until a group of students took it apart and couldn't work out how to put it back together again. (Catherine Cox)

A prank which really did take place happened at Clare Bridge. This is the oldest bridge on the Cam and is adorned with large stone balls along the parapet. In the 1990s one of the balls suffered damage and was taken away to be repaired. While it was missing, several mischievous students made a copy out of papier mâché. They held it in place of the real ball and waited for a punt full of Japanese tourists to pass underneath. Waving down to them, the students then slowly rolled the ball off the bridge, heaving and grunting as if it were very heavy. Seeing this, the tourists (along with their expensive cameras) quickly abandoned ship and swam for safety. They were more than a little vexed to see the ball bounce off their boat into the river and float away serenely.

You will certainly come across some professional chauffeurs and hear their stories. Please take them with a pinch of salt. Some chauffeurs push their stories to the point of absurdity to see what their customers will believe. It is common to hear a gullible American told that 'Jesus studied at Jesus College' or that the greenhouse in St John's gardens is 'so old that the glass panes were originally wooden'. Sometimes it is not the naivety of the customers but the fact they do not speak a word of English. One of my most memorable moments on the river was overhearing a fellow chauffeur amusing himself by intoning to his boatload of Chinese tourists, '… and the rods at the top of King's Chapel are there to attract lightning. They capture it and form it into a giant ball of electricity. It is a marvellous sight. However, it will eventually earth itself and many a student has been injured or even killed in the process. This is why you see so many "keep off the grass" signs in the college.'

RUSTICATION

At any institution there is a need for punishments and Cambridge is no different. The catch-all offence most often cited against pranksters is 'bringing the University into disrepute'. If a prank is serious enough the police may get involved, but in general the University prefers to

The Clare Bridge prank. (Catherine Cox)

settle its problems in-house. Dispensing discipline is a role given to the proctors, and there is a long history to the position. Charters granted by Elizabeth I and James I gave powers to the proctors, not only over members of the University, but over anyone in Cambridge thought to be *personas de male suspectas*. Such undesirables (often prostitutes) could be imprisoned or banished from the city by the proctors without the involvement of the police. This seems strange as a certain level of prostitution seems to have always been tolerated by the University. In fact, many college buildings are adorned with carvings which once advertised them as brothels. The proctors themselves are assisted by 'bulldogs' – sturdy men, often ex-forces, who are sworn in as special constables. There are many stories of clashes between pranksters and bulldogs, as we will later see.

Students have it a little better than townsfolk. Their punishments generally fall into one of three categories. The least severe is 'gating' where the student is confined to his college after a certain hour for a number of days. For middling offences the punishment is 'rustication'

Carvings on Magdalene indicating Cambridge's red light district. (Jamie Collinson)

(from *rusticorum* meaning 'among the heathens'), in which he is suspended from his college for a period of time. This would usually be at least a term. In the most serious cases a student may be 'sent down' and expelled from the University permanently. A long-standing but now mostly defunct tradition was to hold mock funerals for any student sent down. His friends would send a hansom cab to pick up the 'body' at his college and hold a procession through town to the railway station. At the station the 'body' would be placed in the guard's van and he would leave Cambridge forever. The funerals were popular events and attracted large crowds. The theme was also carried into other University occasions. In 1892, a boat procession watched by 10,000 people included a Lady Margaret eight manned by only three rowers dressed in mourning. In the five remaining seats were placards reading 'SENT DOWN' – the rest of the crew had been expelled for making a bonfire in the New Court.

In 1920 the Emmanuel Insurance Society was formed in order that students be able to cover the risk of being punished. A premium of 2s 6d meant that any fine given to him by the University would be repaid. A premium of 10s would cover all fines and also provide a dinner, mock funeral and first-class ticket to his home town should he be sent down. The society flourished until it was featured in a national newspaper. The founder of the society was summoned before the Senior Proctor and asked how he dare treat the University regulations with such contempt. Dismissing the argument that the society expressly advised its members to obey the statutes, the Senior Proctor seemed keen to give out a harsh punishment. However, one of his colleagues, a Pro-Proctor, served on the board of the society and so a fine of £1 was issued and business continued as usual.

MAY WEEK

Many a tourist has been perplexed when visiting the city in June to be told that the drunken students in the streets are celebrating May Week.

May week did originally take place during May, before the year-end exams. As far as I have been able to surmise, this was imagined as a way to improve performance by relaxing before exams. However, progressive educational ideas have forced students to now wait until after exams to let off some steam, and so we are left with the confusing name.

May Week starts with 'Suicide Sunday', named because of the copious amounts of alcohol consumed on the first day on which no one has an exam. It begins a week full of May Balls, garden parties and mayhem. The garden parties are typically run by college drinking societies. There are too many to name individually but special mention goes to the amusingly named Sidney Loving and Giving Society (SLAGS). They always remind me of a friend who wanted to start a punting company called Cambridge University Nautical Tours.

Clare Bridge decorated for a May Ball. (Jamie Collinson)

A famous (and perhaps fictional) May Week prank occurred on the Great Court of Trinity one May Week. Many tourists were inside the college admiring the buildings when they noticed a student walking across the lawns in spite of the vehement 'keep off the grass' signs. Sensing some entertainment, several stopped to watch the hapless undergraduate, who had just been spotted by a college porter. 'Get off the grass!' shouted the porter. The student ignored him and continued nonchalantly. 'Right!' said the porter, and swiftly drew a pistol and fired at the student, who fell to the ground with a scream. The shocked tourists stood slack-jawed, not knowing what to do. After a few moments the undergraduate stood up and the porter removed his costume – he was a student too and it had all been a joke. This is an oft-told story but I have been unable to find any written account.

The balls are always a source of fun. For a certain type of student there is no greater thrill than sneaking into the expensive (currently £100-£200 per ticket) events. Stories of daring entrances abound but the most famous must be the tale of students in dry-suits and scuba tanks diving beneath the surface of the Cam to get into Trinity May Ball. On arriving at the bank, they unzipped their suits, dropped the equipment, and stepped into the ball feeling every bit like James Bond. The story is possibly apocryphal. As any experienced student will tell you, the trick isn't getting into the ball, it's staying inside. Nowadays all tickets come with a wristband which will be checked as you walk between courtyards. While I was an undergraduate some friends broke into Caius with a simple ladder against the wall. They were caught multiple times and ejected but simply went back to the wall and climbed over again. If you're thinking of trying this, take a hint from an old hand – write to the companies which make wristbands asking for samples in various colours. On the night, select whichever colour the ball is using, it will usually work.

Keep off the Grass! (Catherine Cox)

FORMAL HALLS

During term the highlight of the week is often a formal hall. Here the college puts on dinner with table service instead of the usual self-service cafeteria-style meals. Depending on the college, there will be three or four a week which any student can sign up for. They are a cheap way to have a three-course meal, and a fixture of the social calendar. Most colleges require formal dress and gown.

They are often an event with much drinking and joking. A perennial game (often banned but never eliminated) is to 'penny' another student's glass. Since the penny holds an image of the Queen, he or she must quickly drink their wine to prevent her from drowning and thus show their patriotism. It is worrying how clean the penny will be afterwards. This is a quick way to get very drunk and should be treated with caution. This emphasis on alcohol is nothing new. Samuel Taylor Coleridge wrote to a friend of Cambridge undergraduate drunkenness in 1792:

> I add a postscript on purpose to communicate a joke to you. A party of us had been drinking wine together, and three or four freshmen were most deplorably intoxicated. (I have too much respect for delicacy to say drunk.) As we were returning homewards, two of them fell into the gutter (or kennel). We ran to assist one of them, who very generously stuttered out as he lay sprawling in the mud: 'N-n-n-no – n-n-no! – save my f-fr-fr-friend there; n-never mind me, I can swim!'

Coleridge was not the only historical figure with a penchant for wine. An entry dated 21 October 1653 in the Magdalene College Registrar mentions the great Samuel Pepys:

> Pepys and Hind were solemnly admonished by myself and Mr. Hill, for having been scandalously over-served with drink ye night before.

A typical formal hall at St John's. (Jamie Collinson)

It must also be noted that drunkenness was not always confined to the students. R.J. White in *Cambridge Life* reported that:

> Thirty years ago, every undergraduate heard in his first year of the college tutor who was discovered sitting in the middle of a lawn under an umbrella after a Bumps Supper night announcing that he was a mushroom, or of the lecturer who was discovered by his class sitting in a hip-bath with another bath on his head announcing that he was an oyster.

At Caius they have an unusual rule that gowns must be worn to dinner, but formal clothes underneath are optional. This has often led to students dining in swimming costumes and gowns. At Pembroke the formal halls are famous for being candlelit. At all colleges it is usual for the fellows to leave hall before undergraduates, who will often stay to finish their drinks for half an hour or so. Previously the Pembroke candles remained lit for this – until one student decided to demonstrate the explosive properties of finely ground powders (by sprinkling pepper on the candles). The resulting fireballs and smoke means that the college now extinguishes the candles immediately after the fellows leave.

An 1897 banquet in honour of several judges and held by the Vice Chancellor at Downing College was the stage for a prank reported in the *Daily Mail*. After dinner, the judges retired to an adjacent room with a single door which opened inwards. Seeing this, a group of students tied the door handle in such a way that the door could open a few inches but no more. Tugging and tugging, the judges were trapped. One put his hand through and tried to cut the rope with a carving knife, only to have it painted red by the pranksters. Luckily the *Mail* reported that the 'distinguished guests took this practical joke in good part'.

Judges trapped in Downing College. (Catherine Cox)

Another prank is to bring someone/something unusual into hall. In 1932 it was reported that several years previously undergraduates at Emmanuel took a donkey dressed in cap and gown to dinner. The paper remarked that 'most of the aged dons mistook him for one of themselves!' Unfortunately we have no further details of the escapade.

A donkey at Emmanuel formal hall. (Catherine Cox)

More recently, in 1959, Christ's College was subject to a prank by a third-year medical student at Girton named Elizabeth Grant. Wishing to protest the college regulations that women be banned from hall, she attended a dinner completely unnoticed, despite being a twenty-one-year-old blonde. She sat amongst the 200 other students dressed in a grey suit, waistcoat and fake beard, and though there were some odd looks, nobody said a word.

RAGS

At most universities undergraduate rags to raise money for good causes are a time-honoured tradition, and Cambridge is no different. Though now rag might be more associated with students collecting money in buckets, for a long time it was concerned with public stunts and pranks. The 1920s were the heyday of these rags, as the bright young people of the University tried to forget the horrors of the First World War.

A Saturday in 1921 saw the strange sight of hundreds of undergraduates sitting on the pavements of the city centre. This was the inaugural meeting of the Cambridge University Pavement Club. It had previously been publicised with notices sent to many students informing them that the motto of the club was that 'Sitting is the Seat of All Enjoyment' and that they would sit on the city's pavements at noon on each Saturday of Easter Term and engage in 'entertainment, quiet conversation and the reading of newspapers aloud.' A barrel organ had been arranged for this first meeting but was soon moved on by the police. This did not dampen members' spirits and they sat in their hundreds, the clever ones brought cushions and many played cards, marbles, shove ha'penny or tiddlywinks. Before long the proctor arrived with his bulldogs and began taking names for punishment. Those nearby quickly stood up, waited for him to pass, and then sat down again. Undergraduate numbers grew and grew until the organisers decided to conclude the meeting as it was stopping traffic in the streets. The crowd sang 'Auld Lang Syne' and went back about their business.

Bicycle polo.
(Catherine Cox)

One of the better-known Cambridge rags occurred in 1922 when students on bicycles almost caused a riot on King's Parade with their game of bicycle polo. The bicycle-men arrived hidden in a crowd of students, then burst forth wielding hockey sticks and began their game.

Cheers from onlookers soon brought a huge crowd and the centre of town came to a standstill. The game continued for some time until police arrived and confiscated the tennis ball used as the 'pill'. Local papers commented that, 'although not what it might have been it was amusing, which is one point in its favour.'

Also in 1922 was a spectacular rag in which the underground toilets in Market Square were transformed into the tomb of Toot-an-kum-in for a day. Students dressed up and the crowds were treated to the arrival of Cleopatra and fights between Egyptian soldiers before the tomb was opened. Then proud undergraduates emerged clutching lost treasures, culminating in Phineas, the figure of a Scottish Highlander which served as the mascot to University College Hospital in London. Phineas was usually chained up outside Catesby's on Tottenham Court Road, and was only moved when the hospital required him as a rugby mascot. A team of twenty-seven had travelled from Cambridge and secured the door of Catesby's before unchaining Phineas and bundling him into a taxi. It was a celebrated rag and after being unveiled at the tomb, Phineas was sent back to London by train.

On 9 March 1925 a rag was organised in aid of Addenbrooke's Hospital, which was similar to the Tomb of Toot-an-kum-in rag but this time the main event would be the unveiling of a statue of Eros. A large pedestal was set up in the Market Square for the ceremony, but before the unveiling hordes of students in various costumes entertained the crowds. By all accounts, the favourite was an archery contest between the followers of Robin Hood and those of Hengist and Horsa. This done, Henry VIII arrived on a sedan chair carried by beefeaters and followed by Cardinal Wolsey. Henry removed the canvas covering the statue, and the crowd gasped at Eros. He was played by O.M.H. Harmsworth of Pembroke, a stout eighteen-stone undergraduate dressed in red bathing costume, pink tights and little white angel wings.

The tomb of Toot-an-kum-in. (Catherine Cox)

THE OLDEST CAMBRIDGE PRANK?

'Oldest and Smallest of the Cambridge Colleges' is the proud claim of Peterhouse. It may also be the college with the oldest recorded prank. Amongst its lofty alumni Peterhouse counts the poet Thomas Gray. A sombre member of the 'Graveyard Poets', he favoured works on death, mortality, and the finality and sublimity of the end of life. His masterpiece, 'Elegy Written in a Country Churchyard' introduced several popular phrases to the English language, including 'kindred spirit', 'celestial fire' and 'far from the madding crowd'. As befitted one of the predominant poets of the mid-eighteenth century, he was offered the post of Poet Laureate, but refused. A private individual, he preferred solitude and the quiet life of an academic suited him well. He returned to Peterhouse, his *alma mater*, and took up a fellowship.

He led a content enough existence, spending much of his time in his third-floor rooms overlooking the street and churchyard of Little St Mary's. By all accounts, apart from his poetry, Gray had but one love and one fear. The love was one for port, in which he was described as having a 'very pretty taste … but it did not suffice to make him more clubbable [literally, 'suitable for membership of a club' i.e. sociable]'.

His fear was fire. As might be deduced from his works, Gray was obsessed with death but not necessarily frightened of it. Fire, however, grew to be a morbid fear. At Peterhouse he had installed horizontal metal bars above his window-frame. Next to them he kept a coil of rope, so that in case of fire he could tie it to the bars and let himself down. This was a matter of common knowledge at Peterhouse and, combined with his unpopular demeanour, led to a cruel prank. Several students took advantage of his fear by placing a tub of water underneath his window during one cold winter night. They retired to a suitable viewing position and began to cry 'Fire! Fire!' Sure enough, they saw the window flung open and Gray, clad in his nightgown and cap, descended the rope into the waiting tub of icy water. This delighted the students but incensed Gray, who would never forgive the college.

Close up of Gray's window. (Jamie Collinson)

The window bars Thomas Gray had installed at Peterhouse. (Jamie Collinson)

An account from the time in a letter by Revd John Sharp on 12 March 1756 suggests that the well-told story may have been embellished and that there was no tub of water:

Mr Gray, our elegant Poet, and delicate Fellow Commoner of Peterhouse, has just removed to Pembroke-Hall, in resentment of some usage he met with at the former place. The case is much talked of, and is this. He is much afraid of fire, and was a great sufferer in Cornhill; he has ever since kept a ladder of ropes by him, soft as the silky cords by which Romeo ascended to his Juliet, and has had an iron machine fixed to his bedroom window. The other morning, Lord Percival and some Petreuchians, going a-hunting were determined to have a little sport before they set out, and thought

The poet Gray was subject to a rather cruel prank. (Catherine Cox)

it would be no bad diversion to make Gray bolt, as they called it, so ordered their man Joe Draper to roar out fire. A delicate white night-cap is said to have appeared at the window: but finding the mistake, retired again to the couch. The young fellows, had he descended, were determined, they said, to have whipped the butterfly up again.

Whatever the case, it is clear that so terrible was the experience that Gray immediately quit his post at Peterhouse and took a fellowship at Pembroke College, across the street, and still overlooking his beloved churchyard. The bars at Peterhouse remain to this day.

TWO

THINGS ON KING'S

THE NIGHT CLIMBERS

The night climbers are an interesting phenomenon in the history of Cambridge pranks. Many assume that they are a University society in the traditional sense with a committee and register of members. Nothing could be further from the truth – there is no official night climbing society, just collections of individual climbers throughout the ages. The subject often comes to prominence when some object is left atop one of the city's spires, leading to the belief that the climber's aim is always to leave some object on the rooftops. Again this is false; some do but most do not. While the thrill of leaving a clue to their activities for the world to see is attractive, for many it is enough to simply know they have walked where few others dared. Their satisfaction comes from the sheer joy of climbing and the beauty of the college rooftops by moonlight. There is, however, one creed shared by all night climbers: cause no damage to the buildings and don't get caught.

The tradition dates back at least to the eighteenth century, when a student made his mark at a location known amongst climbers as Gunning's Balcony. A lead slab on the roofs of St John's College contains the inscription, 'Petrus Gunning Eliensis, Huius Coll: Alumnus Feb: 19th 1734', which translates as 'Peter Gunning of Ely: student of this college: Feb 19th 1734'. Gunning was the cousin of the Master of St John's and the earliest known night climber. Further evidence from the eighteenth century exists in Trinity College, where various initials and dates have been etched onto the large window at the rear of the Master's Lodge.

Of these early climbers the most famous is Lord Byron. A legend in his own time at Trinity, Byron is most famous amongst Trinitymen for a stunt he played in 1807. Upon being told that he was not permitted to keep a dog while at college, Byron requested a copy of the statutes on forbidden pets. After examining the list and finding several omissions he purchased a tame bear, which was kept tied up outside his rooms, terrifying the college staff. It was not long before the statutes were changed to prohibit every conceivable creature. By all accounts Byron loved the animal, and wrote to Elizabeth Pigot on 26 October 1807:

> I have got a new friend, the finest in the world, a tame bear. When I brought him here, they asked me what I meant to do with him, and my reply was 'he should sit for a fellowship'. This answer delighted them not.

He was also known to be a great climber, reputed to be the first to climb the Great Court Fountain, and also having scaled the Wren Library to decorate the statues.

The Trinity fountain, which Byron was the first to climb. (Jamie Collinson)

The Wren Library statues, which Byron decorated. (Jamie Collinson)

However, it was not until the late nineteenth century that night climbing became well known. It was an era in which mountaineering in the Swiss Alps was popular and, inspired by the mountaineering guides published for tourists, one student wrote the *Roof Climber's Guide to Trinity* in 1900 for a May Week joke. The student was Geoffrey Winthrop Young and could be considered the father of modern night climbing. His book was published anonymously and instantly became a hit amongst undergraduates. A very practical volume, the book details routes up and over the Trinity rooftops, and is much more guidebook than history book. It was flattered with a similar *Roof Climber's Guide to St John's* in 1921, written by some John's undergraduates and published under the name 'A. Climber'. Young was delighted and attended a meeting with the authors to go over the climbing routes.

However, the most famous work on the subject is undoubtedly *The Night Climbers of Cambridge*, which soon became the night climbing bible. It was written by Noel Symington in 1937 and published under the pseudonym 'Whipplesnaith'. The book is well illustrated with flash photographs of his friends attempting the routes. Two of the men featured are Nares Craig and Colin O'Hara Murray (see page 48). It was this book which elevated the night climbers to the status of romantic heroes. As Symington wrote:

> While mountaineers are counted by the tens of thousands, roof-climbers could scarcely be mustered by the dozen. Like characters from Buchan crossing a Scottish moor on a stormy night, they are silent and solitary, mysterious and unknown except to their own circle, preferring to live their own epics to reading those of others.

Most of the tales of the night climbers are impressive but fairly similar – a building is scaled and something left there to the consternation of the college. However, there are a number of incidents which stand out. One well-known case is the statue of Henry VIII above the Great Gate at Trinity. Originally carrying sceptre and orb, the statue has long been targeted by climbers. The sceptre has been removed so many times that the college has given up providing replacements and now leaves a chair leg in the royal hand. In 1932 some climbers on a day out in St Ives carried out a similar prank. They ascended the statue of Oliver Cromwell on the Market Hill and attached a yo-yo to the pointing finger of his outstretched arm. Another favourite from the same year is the tale of two umbrellas placed on the pinnacles of the Trinity Chapel. The college Master knew that one of his students was a crack shot with a rifle and asked him to shoot the umbrellas down. He did so easily, but that night a pair of Union Jack flags appeared in their place. Again the Master called on the rifleman, but this time he was turned down, 'Sir, I couldn't possibly fire at our national flag!' In 1949 a bicycle was placed on the weather vane in Downing Place at the Cambridge School of Geography. Local papers enjoyed this stunt as they wryly observed

Cromwell's yo-yo. (Catherine Cox)

that the practical joker 'apparently thought it would be a good idea to give the meteorologists a new weather cycle.'

Along with Gunning's Balcony there are several other locations which have special names among the climbing fraternity. Once such is a corner of the Trinity Great Court known as 'Sandy's Drop'. It was named after one young man named Sandy Robinson had been celebrating the success of his boat in the Lent Bumps (this was sometime between 1958 and 1960). Returning to his room rather worse for wear, he heard noises on the roof outside. Looking out and above him, he saw four climbers on the parapet and in exuberant mood decided to join them. Making it halfway up the drainpipe he suddenly cried out, 'I'm not going to make it!' and crashed loudly into the shrubbery below. In one of the first-floor windows a light came on and the window opened, followed shortly by one of the dons poking out his head. 'What was the noise?' he shouted into the night. A friend of Sandy's had been watching from his window below and quickly answered, 'That was only Robinson falling out of bed, sir.'

'But it sounded like a very heavy fall,' said the don.

'Yes sir, that's because Robinson is a very heavy sleeper, sir!' replied the quick-witted friend.

Of all the places a night climber can reach, there is one that crowns his career. King's Chapel is the apotheosis of night climbing and no aspiring student of the vertical can be content until he has touched a lightning rod atop one of the spires. Though it has long been subject to the placement of small objects among the pinnacles, chiefly chamber pots, flags, umbrellas and gowns, more recently the objects have taken a more political bent. This can be traced back at least to 1937 and George VI's coronation. Two night climbers from Trinity and Emmanuel, Nares and O'Hara, took it upon themselves to place an effigy of the soon-to-be king upon the chapel. After a trip to Woolworth's to purchase a boiler suit, which was duly stuffed with hay, the pair planned to suspend this up between the two pinnacles facing onto King's Parade. A crown strung a few feet above the head and a beer bottle with mug for the hands would complete the spectacle.

Henry VIII's chair leg. (Jamie Collinson)

They got the dummy up onto the rooftop without incident. From here the plan was to use ropes and a pulley to haul it up between the spires. As they began to pull, it was evident that one thing had been forgotten – oil for the pulley. It caused such a squeaking that the college began to wake, including the porter on duty at the front gate. Hurriedly they tied off the rope with the effigy suspended, but had no time to raise the crown. They had no choice but to flee from the rooftop, where they were being watched carefully by the porter. O'Hara was a large and strong young man, and told his friend Nares to run for the backs while he slowed down the porter. Nares fled towards the river as O'Hara wrestled with the porter on the college lawn. Nares, curious as to O'Hara's condition, turned back towards the college only to see a porter on a bicycle bearing down on him. By now close to the river, he had little choice but to dive in. This proved useless as an escape route and he was fished out shortly afterwards.

Dragged before the Dean, one dripping wet and the other red with exhaustion and trouserless, it seemed certain that they would be sent down for the prank. However, Nares was a favourite of a well-known chaplain at Trinity, who persuaded the University to reduce the sentence to a term's rustication. On returning after the summer break, Nares discovered that the college had placed spikes on the rooftop to deter future climbers. However, they were ineffective – several climbers were still attempting the chapel, although a few had already had minor accidents. Visiting the Dean, he offered to make the climb impossible. The Dean agreed and soon the spikes were removed and instead large chock-stones were placed in the four corner gaps which climbers used. This put a stop to the best-known route to the top of the chapel – grasping one of the lightning conductors, placing one's back against the wall, feet against a buttress and inching up to the roof.

However, where there's a will, there's a way and before long climbers were experimenting with a new route, and perfected a way up on the north of the chapel, facing the Senate House and Caius. This is not the place for a detailed 'how to' guide, but anyone sufficiently interested can look it up in one of the several guidebooks. In the summer of 1965 politically charged students decided to put up a banner protesting the war in Vietnam. Knowing full well of the aborted attempt in 1936 to hang a 'SAVE ETHIOPIA' banner (though a Union Jack and Abyssinian flag were successfully placed), it was not a simple task.

Three experienced night climbers volunteered for the job, and their first problem was the construction of a suitable banner. The Ethiopian attempt had failed because the banner was too heavy and apt to catch the wind. As a result, it was torn by gusts before it could be secured in place. Advances in technology since the 1930s had made new materials available. This banner would be made of a white mesh with black tape sewn on for lettering, and it would be suspended by light but strong nylon cord rather than heavy rope or wire. The banner was prepared in Girton (then a girls-only college) and kept under a young lady's bed until it was needed. Though word got out about its construction, no one knew where it was to be placed, and Girton is a long way from the centre of Cambridge. The plan remained secret.

After several practise climbs and much unsung work by sewing Girtonians everything was ready. Sunday, 6 June 1965 was to be the night of the climb. Several lookouts were selected to watch the porter's lodge and patrolling policemen, and the operation began at about 1.45 a.m. on the Monday morning. Coming across the backs into King's sent a shiver down the climbers' spines; in the darkness they could see the enormous chapel looming. They had climbed it before, but never with such a grand scheme in mind. The conditions were less than perfect. Their practise climbs had been during a spell of warm and dry weather, but Sunday had brought rain. The old stones were mossy and became slick at the slightest moisture. Two of the climbers wore klets and found them useless in these conditions; the other never climbed in anything but his usual shoes and found them to grip just as well as usual.

Following the slippy but successful climb to the roof, one student laid out the banner between the pinnacles, while the other two prepared to climb them. They would each head up one of the spires trailing a 60ft length of nylon string which passed from one to the other and through the banner. Once aloft they would shorten their lengths to haul the banner up between the spires. As they neared the top disaster almost struck. Below a burglar alarm went off and all three froze. Had they been spotted? After a few tense moments the lookouts signalled that all was clear – the alarm had likely been set off by several foreign girls climbing out of King's, a common enough occurrence. With relief, the two on the spires tied off their strings to the lightning rods and looked for confirmation from the lookouts to begin the hoist. After five or six minutes waving their arms at the top of the spires they realised that they were now too high to be seen against the night sky and, getting sore from the tricky holds, decided to haul the banner up.

The banner was excellently designed and due to its lightness flew up with ease. Tying it off was not so simple at such a height. Balanced on dangerous footing, the pair secured the nylon cord with knot after knot. Finally happy, they descended a few feet and admired their handiwork. They had been nearly half an hour on the climb, with twenty of those minutes spent atop the pinnacles, but the results were worth it. Floating gently between them was the huge banner, 38ft long by 5ft high, proclaiming 'PEACE IN VIETNAM'. With the job done, the two descended further to the roof and met the third man. He had not been idle, after freeing the banner from tangles on its ascent he had laid out ropes ready for a quick descent. Expertly they abseiled down the side of the chapel and shot off into the night. It was 3.15 a.m.

At around 4 a.m. a policeman on his night patrol looked up and spotted the banner. Radioing back to station he was soon joined by a squad car and three colleagues. They knocked on the door of the porter's lodge and enquired, 'Here, mate, have you seen your chapel?' A rude awakening for the porter, but all soon realised there was nothing to be done until daybreak and the police drove off while the porter went back to bed. By lunchtime there was only one subject of discussion in Cambridge and the culprits found it difficult to keep their silence. They sent a letter to the Dean of King's:

We would like to inform you, on the basis of our experiences last night, of the very dangerous condition of the stonework on the pinnacles of your chapel. We suggest that unless restoration work is carried out immediately, the safety of future climbers of your chapel is in grave jeopardy.

A santa hat on King's. (Catherine Cox)

Reactions to the prank were mixed. One American tourist was seen jumping up and down in anger, shouting, 'Communists! Communists!' Though as a whole the University seemed to see the joke. The Domus Bursar at King's told the press that 'it was a very good climb. In the past we have had balloons, chamber pots and umbrellas on the pinnacles, but nothing like this.' After some BBC interviews in which the identity of the climbers was badly disguised it became well known who was behind the prank, but punishment did not arrive. The Head Porter came to see two of the climbers and told them proudly, 'I was watching the telly with my wife last night, and a

Another hat appeared on Clare chapel. (Catherine Cox)

programme came on about the banner on King's Chapel. "Here," I said, "they're my boys.'"

It was certainly not the last time that King's was targeted. Since the Vietnam banner, many have climbed the chapel and left their mark in the form of a rooftop umbrella, traffic cone or other piece of detritus. A particularly nice variation was played in the winter of 2009 when pranksters climbed all four pinnacles and placed Father Christmas hats atop each spire. The college was less than pleased as they were forced to hire steeplejacks to take the hats down. It took them two days and several thousand pounds. I doubt it will be the last time a night climber takes a trip up to the top of the chapel …

CUBES

Alongside the night climbers are a little-known group known as the Cambridge University Breaking and Entering Society (Cubes). Their passion is not strictly for climbing, but to gaining access to the places in which students are forbidden. To them a locked door is a challenge to which the only reasonable response is to break in and leave a note indicating that the room in question has been 'cubed'. Pride is taken in never causing damage or being detected, and in always locking up after they leave. The best loved of the Cubes' accomplishments has been ongoing for many years. In 1986 they broke into the supposedly well secured dining hall of Trinity College. The customary note was eschewed in favour of an unusual calling card – a decoy duck stolen from the Mallards dining society and wedged between the wooden beams of the vaulted roof.

At first the Master and fellows were fairly ambivalent to the interloper watching them at mealtimes, but soon grew tired of guests and tourists asking about the duck's significance. Contractors were hired and removed it with some difficulty. Unfortunately for the college by this time the mallard was well liked amongst the student body and was soon replaced. Since then it has come, gone and moved around the rafters frequently, but is present more often than not. In recent years it has appeared with a remote-controlled electronic 'quacker', and also as a yellow rubber duck.

The Trinity Duck in the rafters of Trinity Dining Hall. (Catherine Cox)

Next time you visit Cambridge take the opportunity to look up; you might see something inspired by the Night Climber's Anthem (to the tune of the Red Flag):

> The heights by great men reached and kept
> Were not attained by sudden flight,
> But they while their companions slept
> Were toiling upwards through the night.

> 'Excelsior' shall be our cry,
> We'll never stop, we'll never tire,
> Until at last we see on high
> A chamber-pot on every spire!

THE AUSTIN SEVEN

Of all the night climbing escapades there is one which stands out above all others. To pranksters the world over Cambridge is synonymous with this particular stunt, perpetrated during the hectic May Week of June 1958. It was a prank to inspire a generation of tricksters and many copycat schemes. There is simply something wonderful about putting something large somewhere it was never intended to be, especially when it is truly a challenge and all goes to plan.

It must have been a very strange sight on the morning of Sunday, 8 June 1958 as Cambridge woke from the restless slumber of a night filled with college balls, food, wine, music and excitement at the end of the exam season. An observer walking along Cambridge's iconic King's Parade would have seen a small huddle of people atop the old library adjacent to the bright white Senate House. (The Senate House is a building of great importance to every Cambridge student as it is the place their exam results are publicly posted and where their degree ceremony is held.)

The huddlers were gazing in amazement across the roof to the apex of Senate House. There sat the unlikely spectacle of an elderly black Austin Seven van. The van was battered and had clearly suffered during its ascent, but it was complete and its shape was instantly recognizable. The group soon grew and by six in the morning there sat three policemen, a professional photographer in full morning dress and three young people – two plimsolled male undergraduates looking the worse for wear and a shivering under-dressed girl.

As you have probably guessed, the young people were not innocent spectators. At least one of them was a core member of the team of perpetrators. Like any conspiracy, there were many involved in the process but the prank really belonged to a small subgroup – in this case four friends with an engineering bent.

It had all begun during the previous May Week, when four students – Davey, Jacobs, Balchin and Roberts – pondered how best to spend the last few nights of term. Roberts was a year above the other three and Davey proposed a prank as celebration of Roberts' final year. He could not help but think that a motor vehicle parked on one of the roofs along King's Parade would make for a very striking image. At the time it seemed an attractive yet unfeasible scheme and the friends settled for a less spectacular outing, stealing a 6ft by 4ft traffic diversion sign and then placing it on the rooftops. This was certainly no mean feat but was also not unusual. Tastes among night climbers change with time but by the twentieth-century traffic signs had become a firm favourite.

In the intervening year this grand scheme – to hoist a motorcar onto the rooftops of Cambridge – took root in the minds of the remaining three. They studied for the Mechanical Sciences Tripos and the idea of putting their learning to practical use, along with the spectacle it would cause, must have been beguiling.

Senate House was decided on as the perfect place to park a rooftop vehicle. Its advantages were many. Anything placed on its roof would be in full view of King's Parade; it was a Cambridge landmark and thus held prestige as a target; Senate House Passage could serve as cover for the hoist; the group were based in Tree Court of Caius College, adjacent to the Senate House, and so had the option to access the Senate House rooftops from the top of the court battlements. The choice of vehicle was simple. Austins were ubiquitous in post-war Britain, they were also small, light, simple cars — the Austin weighed less than half as much as a T Ford.

However, using Senate House as a target was not without its difficulties. Three key problems were identified and would need to be solved before the plan could be completed. First was how to reach the rooftops. Though they had access — one of the group had rooms in the battlement turret of Tree Court — this was usually achieved by the notorious leap across the Senate House Passage, a good 6ft gap, 70ft above the ground. Hardly a convenient way to transport the lifting materials which would be needed, and a difficult sell to the fellow students they would need to carry out the lift.

Second was the overhanging ledge and 4ft banister which would make it difficult to manoeuvre a lifted object onto the roof after it had been hoisted to the top of the building. This was something the engineers would have to overcome with their design for a lifting mechanism.

Third, the Austin Seven would have to be placed in the Senate House Passage after dark, ready to be lifted. To make the hoist easier, and to prevent the car damaging the Senate House roof, it would be necessary to strip the car for lightness. As a result, the problem was how to get the car into the centre of Cambridge undetected after its engine and rear axle had been removed. As this would require some extensive modifications, the plotters decided that they would need to purchase an old Austin Seven and work on it somewhere private, rather than borrow it for the night.

They calculated that, after lightening, the car would weigh between 600lb and 800lb (270kg – 360kg). A permanent structure would have given the game away, so whatever lifting apparatus was to be used would have to be assembled and then dismantled on the night of the hoist. A simple plank bridge over the Senate House Passage would be

Senate House Passage. (Jamie Collinson)

used to get six men onto the roof from Caius College, where they would then assemble the equipment and carry out the lift.

An appropriate lifting mechanism was crucial to the success of the plan and the pranksters gave it much thought. It had to be a simple design, easy to assemble quickly and silently in the dark. It would also be required to withstand substantial force; they could not countenance a collapse during the operation. Davey, Jacobs and Balchin knew that if they miscalculated then they, their friends, and passers-by could be seriously injured. Not to mention any damage to the surrounding buildings.

Eventually they decided on a simple triangular derrick. It would consist of two 16ft scaffolding poles joined together at one end to form a 24ft high triangle. The open end would rest on the Senate House roof with the poles held to the rooftop banister by wire straps. It was reckoned that the 12ft gap between the feet would be enough to prevent the construction toppling sideways. Of course, this triangle could not stand up on its own. A steel cable would act as a backstay – connected to the apex of the triangle, it would be strapped to a giant urn decorating the King's College side of the Senate House roof. This cable would initially be left long enough to allow the derrick to lean out over the balcony and above the Senate House Passage. Once the Austin had been hoisted to the top of the passage the backstay cable could be shortened to pull the triangular derrick upright, and the car could then be lowered onto the roof.

In order to prevent any damage to the buildings on the way up, the team were careful to incorporate protective measures into their design. The feet of the derrick would stand on planks on the rooftop. They would be placed far enough from the banister that the car could be lowered onto the flat area between the edge and the derrick. Anywhere that wires were connected to the building sacking would be used to protect the stonework. Finally, steadying lines would be connected to the car itself so that it could be controlled and prevented from swinging around and smashing any windows on the way up.

If all went to plan then a ground party would manoeuvre the Austin into place below the mechanism. They would pull on a line to bring down the hook and tackle from the apex of the derrick. The hook would then be run through a hole cut in the roof of the vehicle for the purpose and attached to a lifting eye bolted to the chassis. Once hooked on, the ground team would move to take the steady lines in the Tree Court of Caius College and give the signal to begin the lift.

With the details of the lifting mechanism in place another problem quickly appeared. Where would the car come from? Buying one was not as simple as it might sound. Austin Sevens were still so popular that none could be found in the area – even amongst the wrecks in the local scrapyards. The best that could be found was a decrepit engineless Austin Seven van, overgrown with nettles in a village several miles south of Cambridge. The van was heavier than the saloon model they had originally intended to use, but there was no other option. They believed that their design would lift a heavier vehicle – but only time would tell.

They purchased the van for £4 10s on the condition that the re-usable parts were returned. This suited the plan perfectly as they had always intended to remove the heavy back axle and rear wheels for the lift. It was no problem to find worn out tyres which could be added to give the illusion of completion once it had ascended Senate House. A month before May Week the van was towed to a farmyard in Coton, to the west of Cambridge, where it could be worked on in privacy. The journey must have been an interesting one for onlookers. Davey's car towed the van, and was only in marginally better shape than the trailing vehicle. The van itself was steered by its previous owner. Davey noted that he did very well considering that the steering gear was chiefly fencing wire.

Upon its arrival in Coton the serious work began. The van would need to be towed into town then manually manoeuvred to the lifting point in the Senate House Passage. Since the owner wanted the back axle it was loosened so that after the tow into town it could be easily removed and sent back to him. Since the van would then have no back wheels, fittings were added to the sides so that short scaffolding poles could be inserted and used to lift the vehicle onto its front wheels. The ground team could then trundle it around like a wheelbarrow.

What little remained in the way of luxuries were stripped from the chassis. Only the components absolutely necessary to get the van into town remained. Externally it would look like a complete but unloved Austin Seven, internally it would be little more than a shell. However, the exterior could not escape completely untouched. The plan called for a hole to be cut in the roof for the lifting hook to pass through. A weighty pyramid made of 3/8inch steel rod was bolted to the chassis to serve as the lifting eye. An important detail here was the position of the eye. The team had no way to be sure of the centre of gravity and had to make do with estimations. If they were wrong the van would not be level on its ascent but would rise nose up or down, causing great difficulties at the top of the building. Though the guide lines could correct for minor errors they would be no help if the placement was out by more than a few inches.

On the evening of 28 May, as term neared its end, two of the team made their way across onto Senate House to make a detailed survey of the terrain. They already knew the layout quite well but for their plan to be successful accurate sketches of the rooftop would be needed. Armed with knotted rope and steel measuring tape, they surveyed the roof in the darkness, making notes on the distances between and measurements of all the rooftop objects. With this information they would make a scale drawing of the rooftop and its environs, correct to within a few inches.

From this drawing they could finalise the dimensions of the derrick and other equipment needed for the lift. Re-checking their earlier calculations based on the new scale drawing confirmed that scaffolding poles would be sufficiently strong to form the sides of the derrick without buckling. Handily enough, a few days later on 31 May some builders at King's College left out some loose scaffolding which would be perfect for the job. That night five 16ft scaffolding poles were smuggled out of King's and into Caius, where they were artfully concealed.

On 2 June, a week before the van was due to be lifted, the poles and accompanying gear were hauled onto the Tree Court roof and passed across to Senate House. This proved a more difficult task than imagined and took much longer than expected, causing Davey and the team to wonder if getting the Austin Seven aloft undetected was an impossible dream.

During these preparations the group had been carefully recruiting from their circle of friends. Their plan could not be completed without the extra manpower, but it was also crucial that all involved could be trusted. If they were found out the conspirators risked police involvement, or worse, being sent down from the University.

Balchin and Jacobs would lead the ground party which would bring the Austin Seven into position. They were joined by a friend whose surname was Brett and two ladies. The lifting party would consist of Davey and Roberts (who had made the trip back to Cambridge from Scotland for the occasion) along with four stout friends – Messrs Usher, Fisher, Dimock and Kidd. Two students named Pritchett and Fowler would be dedicated to operating a drawbridge over the Senate House Passage. This was an unsung but essential role to the smooth running of the operation.

With the team split into parties the plan was also broken down into steps. With each group well briefed on their responsibilities they were also given safe fall-back positions. Should an alarm be raised each group would go to a pre-arranged point, act casually and wait for the all-clear. With luck, this would prevent a false alarm putting a stop to the whole operation. The danger point was during the lift itself. Once the van was mid-air the plan would have to continue until it was on the roof, regardless of any alarms raised. With the local police beats studied and a lookout recruited – in the case of danger he would start a noisy Vespa scooter by Great St Mary's Church, close enough for everyone to hear – the plan was as complete as it would get. All that remained were the final preparations.

To complete the hoist, several further pieces of equipment would be needed for the scaffold pole derrick. The team collected over 250ft of steel wire rope, 200ft of hemp rope, pulley blocks, hooks and tackle. Lastly they added plenty of planks, sacks and light rope – these items would be used to prevent damage to the buildings and cover anything missed in the planning stages. The steel rope was precut and knotted, then coiled and labelled with cardboard so that it could be correctly positioned in the dark – on the night there would be no time to spare for sorting through the derrick components.

On 4 June a party of four crossed over to the roof of Senate House where they constructed and erected the derrick as the final test of the design before the real event. Everything looked good and the lifting mechanism was folded up and hidden out of sight on Senate House roof. The night also served as a practise for crossing over the passage. Caution dictated that each member of the lifting team have a rope tied round their waist for each crossing. They also practised looking ahead as they crossed – a glance down could cause even a brave man to freeze up and slow the team down. By the end of the night everyone had walked the plank drawbridge at least once and some were becoming quite confident with the crossing.

With all prepared, the decision came – which night should be chosen for the actual lift? The end of term was nearing. All exams would be over by the 7th, after which Cambridge would explode into garden parties and May Balls for one week before the student population faded away for the summer. It would make no sense to carry out the prank after May Week, when the audience had dissipated. This left a roughly two-week window of opportunity. May Week itself seemed like a good idea until Davey and Co. realised that the streets would be teeming with night-time revellers – hardly an ideal setting to hoist a van onto the rooftops undetected.

So Saturday 7 June was chosen. It was also the last night of bumps, when each college's rowers would be holding a noisy supper celebration. With any luck, this would serve as good cover for the prank.

The day arrived and all were full of nerves. Many had spent the previous days completing their Tripos examinations and had received little sleep. Much of the plan remained untested and would only be proved achievable if the night went as intended. Would the six men in the roof party have the strength to lift the van? Could the ground party manoeuvre the van correctly into position in the passage? Was the lifting eye central enough to keep the van level as it ascended? If it made it to the flat of the roof could the van be moved to the apex? None of these questions could be answered before the actual lift as testing had been very limited.

Another concern was simply getting the Austin into town. It was now in a very reduced state having been modified and manhandled quite extensively. With the interior stripped and the rear axle barely attached Davey thought it looked more like a stage prop than a road-worthy vehicle. Could it escape unwanted police attention as it was towed into town? Would it even make the journey?

To guard against interference by the authorities Balchin had a stroke of genius – since Davey thought it now looked like a stage prop why not disguise the van as a publicity float for one of the college May Balls? The group chose St Catharine's and made up large posters to cover the Austin's exterior. Now covered with slogans such as 'We're going to get to Cats May Ball – ARE YOU?', the van set off from Coton in the early afternoon. The towing of this gaudily decorated old vehicle must have appeared a very strange publicity stunt, but despite a good deal of attention none questioned the innocence of its arrival in town.

The van was parked by Clare College, at the rear of Senate House and somewhat out of sight. Without hesitation, the team went to work on the Austin. The back end was lifted so that the rear axle could be removed, this proved such an easy task all were surprised it had survived the journey into town without collapse. The driving seat and wheels were also shed, destined to be taken back to the previous owner as agreed. Two old wheels were fitted to the front while the doors were removed. The doors, wrapped in brown paper, were disguised as paintings and joined the similarly wrapped rear wheels, which would be smuggled into Caius as large cushions. The work being done, the van was wrapped in polythene, fitted with a parking light and left in solitude.

Though relieved that the van had made it into town safely, there was much yet to come. As before, the tower room in Tree Court was used as a base camp. By midnight the floor was piled high with rope, planks and pulleys for the operation – not to mention the doors and rear wheels removed from the van. The first task of the night was to move all this equipment across the makeshift bridge to Senate House roof. This fell to Davey and Roberts – more men would be more visible in the twilight and with the bridge as bottleneck would not speed things up significantly. Once the equipment was over they would be joined by the other four members of the lifting party. They would come from another of Tree Court's staircases and then cross over the bridge. As practised, the drawbridge would be raised after crossing to minimize its silhouette, this would leave the hoisting party stranded if there were to be a major alarm, but was considered unavoidable to prevent detection.

No sooner had Davey and Roberts left the safety of the tower room than disaster struck. The equipment they were carrying clattered loudly down the slates of Tree Court, arousing the unwanted attention of policemen patrolling on King's Parade. The Vespa engine was fired as an alarm and the two conspirators were forced back into the tower to avoid being spotted on the roof. Simultaneously the ground party had their own run-in with police investigating a Bentley, which party-goers had got stuck on Garret Hostel Bridge. This was not the smooth start the team had wanted and did not bode well for the plan.

Everyone gathered together to discuss the disastrous start. Several members of the team were ready to give up, particularly those who had encountered the police. The four planners held fast and persuaded the rest to continue – they would wait an hour and begin again. Time was now a real issue. The delay had pushed the start to nearly 2 a.m., and with sunrise before 5 a.m. there would be little room for error. On the positive side, the city was now very quiet and the police less alert –

with post-exam revellers retreated to the colleges they were now the University's problem, not the city's.

The ground party scurried down to the van, removed the cover, and wheelbarrowed it down the passageway to the steps of the Senate House. The lifting party went up to the bridge, leaving three men below to move the van into position and lay out the steady lines. The original plan for Davey and Roberts to transport the equipment alone was abandoned in favour of a group effort to increase speed. This went perfectly and within forty minutes the stores had been moved over and the derrick assembled. The ground party watched it swing out above them over the passageway, then moved the van into position and attached the hook to the chassis through the hole in the roof. They pulled the steady lines tight and with a flutter in their stomachs gave the signal to begin the lift.

The roof party were anxious too. This was the moment of truth. No one had any doubt that six men could take the weight of the Austin – they could probably manage that on the ground with brute force, never mind the mechanical advantage bestowed by the lifting equipment. It was the equipment itself that worried them. What had looked safe enough on the page would now face the reality of lifting the lightened but still substantial van.

Five men began to pull while the sixth looked down into the darkness to spot any problems. As they pulled, the van remained stationary while the tip of the derrick visibly bowed down toward it. Metal and wire screamed in complaint, but after what seemed an age the van inched off the ground and swung gently. Encouraged by this, the five redoubled their efforts and brought the van a few feet higher. Then, with a terrible jerk, the scaffolding lurched as one of the joints slipped. The Austin rapidly retraced its ascent and hit the ground with a crash.

The derrick was re-checked and one joint was found to be loose, presumably missed in the darkness. The sixth man changed role, wrapping the end of the lifting line around a pedestal on the opposite side of the roof. Between hauls he would tighten the line to prevent the van dropping again. The lift resumed and went well. Although the derrick bent significantly, within the space of a few minutes the van was halfway up.

With half the lift complete the roof party were exhausted and tied off the main line to inspect their work. Peering over the edge of the roof they could see the mass of the van below. The two steady lines snaked away from the vehicle; one led further into the Senate House Passage, the other disappeared into Tree Court. Together they allowed just a little movement in the van, which swung eerily in the night air. None could deny it was a magnificent sight.

After a short period of inspection and self-congratulation the team went back to their posts to resume the lift. It was at this point that they realised that they were not alone; beneath the half-hoisted van stood a trio of oarsmen. Considerably worse for wear from the evening's celebrations, they gazed up at the indistinct shape floating above them. They could not fathom what could possibly be levitating behind the Senate House in the early hours of the morning, and were oblivious to the danger which could land on them at any moment. As they reached out to pull on the steady line, putting themselves at great risk, Balchin swooped in and with great quick thinking told them he was tethering a loose weather balloon. Satisfied with this plausible defence, the rowers wandered off to safety.

Excitement abated, the van continued to rise and was soon clear of the roof and then the balustrade. The backstay rope was shortened to bring the apex of the derrick, and the Austin, over the roof. Unfortunately, the van had twisted so that it would not fit between the edge and the derrick frame. Tentatively the team reached up and tried to spin the van. To give it more room, the van was lowered a few feet and pushed towards the frame. As it touched the force was enough to tip the derrick past vertical, removing all support. With painful slowness the whole contraption hinged backwards and then, picking up speed, the van swung through the frame and fell the remaining five feet. Simultaneously the derrick toppled backwards and with a deafening crash both landed in a messy heap on the rooftop.

Senate House, showing the balustrade which caused so much difficulty. (Jamie Collinson)

There stood the team, shaken but luckily having suffered only superficial injuries from the collapse. The van was nearly hidden by the mass of equipment, and worse, dawn was close to breaking. The students went about the final stages quickly. They extracted the van from its ignoble pile and manhandled it up the final slope of the roof to the apex. In the blink of an eye the doors and wheels were refitted and the van was outwardly complete once again. It had not suffered too much in the ascent and from the ground looked as good as ever. The derrick was dismantled and the lighter equipment rushed back over the bridge or thrown onto the lawn below, all to be returned to its owners the following day during the media hubbub. Unfortunately time proved too short to bring the scaffolding down – getting it up had been difficult enough and with day breaking it was piled neatly next to the van.

The Austin Seven prank. (Catherine Cox)

As the drawbridge was pulled back for the last time the prank was complete. The four planners could hardly believe that it had actually succeeded. However, escape was on their minds and there was no time to stop and admire their work. As the last six of the lifting party returned to the safety of Caius they spotted a policeman on his early morning beat, though luckily he did not return their glances and the van remained undetected until they were back to base-camp. The only casualty to the constabulary was one of the ground party, caught gathering up the lines thrown down onto the lawns.

Too late for the Sunday papers, it was not until Monday morning that the press began to have their say about the prank. Then as now, the nationals had a fondness for stories about Cambridge and its students' escapades, and were very happy to feature a story on the frivolity of youth (while displaying a subtext of quiet admiration). Written in haste, many facts were incorrect (one suspects simply made up to fit the story). The *Daily Express* reported that a rowing crew and an engineering student had climbed the outside of the building and hauled the Austin up for a bet with a local publican. *The Times* made the feat seem even more impressive than it was, particularly since they announced that Senate House was a towering 180ft high.

The authorities now faced the daunting task of getting the van back down, an event which was enjoyed as entertainment by many in Cambridge. First the police and fire brigade attempted the problem, getting as far as moving the Austin down from the apex of the roof to the flat part. Next, the Civil Defence Force (CDF) stepped forward, volunteering to bring the van down as an exercise for their men. With little time to prepare, it was a difficult task. All the more so because of an audience of hundreds on the streets.

With the Senate House roof crowded with civic and University bigwigs, and every facing window full with undergraduates and reporters, the CDF operation began. With the pranksters' lifting team replaced by a lorry in the Senate House Passage, they had much more power than Balchin and Davey had dreamed of. Using the scaffolding poles left on the roof from the ascent, a lifting mechanism similar

Members of the Civil Defence Force try unsuccessfully to lower the Austin Seven.
(Photo by Central Press/Hulton Archive/Getty Images)

to the original derrick was created, and the Austin attached to the lorry via a pulley. However, the CDF ran into the same problem as the student team and could not get the van over the balustrade and ledge. Even after some hasty reshaping with a sledgehammer, the best they could manage was resting the Austin precariously on the edge. By Wednesday morning these attempts to lower the van down whole were abandoned. An oxy-acetylene torch was taken up to the rooftop and used to cut the van into six pieces, which were unceremoniously driven away to the scrapyard.

The details of how this incredible feat was carried out were not revealed for five long decades. It was only when several of the planners came clean that the full story could be told. Naturally it was a story of great interest in the media as the original prank garnered many column inches and much amazement throughout the country. It is rare to hear the details of such a student prank from the planners, and any who know the story will not be surprised that these enterprising young men went on to distinguished careers. One was awarded a CBE and honorary doctorate (neither was for the prank) and another became a lieutenant colonel in the British Army.

The Austin Seven prank spawned several copycat stunts including hanging another Austin Seven beneath the Bridge of Sighs in 1963. (Catherine Cox)

The prank was so successful that it has entered popular memory and spawned a few notable copycat stunts. The best conceived was in 1963 when another Austin Seven (this time the saloon model) was punted down the river on four lashed-together punts, and then hoisted up and suspended from the Bridge of Sighs. This was repeated using a Reliant Regal (an older sibling of the infamous Reliant Robin) in 1968.

THREE

A HISTORY OF HOAXES

HORACE DE VERE COLE

The name Horace de Vere Cole may not be well known today, but in his day Cole was famous throughout Britain as an eccentric public figure and prankster. In the early 1920s he was a household name along with people like Marcel Duchamp and Charlie Chaplin. His most famous stunt, the Dreadnought Hoax, would shame the Royal Navy for its hubris, cause political scandal, and spark a new fashion for fancy dress parties. He is still occasionally mentioned by newspapers short of pieces on April Fool's Day, when he is often referred to as the 'King of the Jokers'. However, he was also deeply conflicted. Here was a man who elevated pranks to an art form, but who was perhaps ahead of his time – born before the rise of mass media, he was briefly a star but soon faded into anachronism as his eccentricity teetered on the edge of madness.

Horace's grandfather had little in the way of education, yet with self-made prosperity sent his two sons to Eton, then Trinity College, Cambridge. As the family continued to ascend the social hierarchy, it was clear that Horace, despite a lack of application in his studies, would continue on the same path. Weeks after his mother remarried, Horace was sent off to Eton, a situation which he found objectionable:

> Why the devil, with such a handicap, was I sent to Eton where no deaf boy could hear anything in form? Callous cruelty to a boy with £600 a year, I call it. I should have been taught a trade or profession.

His career at Eton was undistinguished, winning no prizes, playing in no school teams and having no positions of responsibility. Never rising with the clever boys, he stayed in the lower sets alongside Lawrence Oates, who would one day travel to the Antarctic with Captain Scott, and make the ultimate sacrifice. Despite this, Horace did enjoy learning, particularly history, and was also popular with the other boys. Eton ingrained in him the upper-class sensibilities of manners and sportsmanship, qualities which would never leave him even as he turned away from conventional society later in his life.

In February 1900 he left Eton to enlist in the Duke of Cambridge's Own to fight in the Boer War, and by May had arrived in Cape Town as the youngest cavalryman in the whole British Army. He advanced quickly, helped by family connections and mounting losses in his unit. On 2 July, now an acting captain, he was returning from an engagement with the enemy when he was shot by a Boer sniper. He was soon taken to a field hospital and given surgery that would save his life but leave him so that for the rest of his life even taking a heavy fall might kill him. More importantly, this event proved to be the end of his innocence and removed his fear of death. Returning to Britain by hospital ship, his adventure, and any hope of following in the footsteps of his military relatives, was over. After three months of active service all Horace had to show for his endeavours was a campaign medal, an officer's moustache and a pension of £2 per week for his wound. The latter he immediately cashed in for £1,800 and gave to the war widows and orphans fund.

Once recovered sufficiently, Cole set to getting a place at Cambridge. After a period of cramming with a private tutor he took the entrance exams and scraped a pass. In October 1902 he began his first year. Flirting on the edges of the intellectual elite with Oscar Browning's 'Apostles' like Leonard Woolf and John Maynard-Keynes, Horace was also a member of the heavy-drinking Magpie and Stump society, named after a local brothel. Though he had been brought up a Tory, during the war Cole had lived with working-class tommies, and when Fabian Socialism became popular in Cambridge, Cole was quick to convert his ideology. Along with the cynicism which came from seeing the realities of war, it was this turn to a socialist viewpoint which led him to see the establishment, and in particular the Cambridge dons around him, as worthy of ridicule.

Initially serious-minded, Cole engaged in increasing numbers of rags, and as time went on was often the ringleader. He joined the Cambridge Alpine Club and climbed the college roofs at night with Geoffrey Winthrop Young, author of the *Roof Climber's Guide to Trinity*. He also continued the tradition of large fake funerals for friends who were sent down, notably organising one for poet T.E. Hulme. He would slip into the Newmarket to Cambridge walking race and cheat to win by a huge margin, and visit public schools while pretending to be the Bishop of Madras to carry out baptisms and confirmations. As well as these harmless stunts a hint at the darker side of his character was present even at this early stage, a perfect example being when one of his friends woke at 3 a.m. to a drunken Cole playing the crude prank of thrusting a dagger into the pillow either side of his head.

In his second year at Cambridge, Horace moved into college rooms in Neville's Court. It is interesting to note that a few rooms along lived Prince Yugala of Siam – perhaps an exotic inspiration for the prank which was to follow. No longer a freshman student, Horace and his friends sought a grand scheme to occupy themselves. One friend suggested travelling to Alsace-Lorraine, putting on German uniforms and crossing the border into France. Given that the two countries were at odds over control of Morocco, this had the potential to cause a serious international incident, and could well have lead to the perpetrators being shot. It was not this risk that Horace objected to – he simply thought it too impractical and costly, one also suspects from his other escapades that he was a man who liked an audience, and his countrymen would be too far removed from a hoax on foreign shores.

Instead, he proposed something closer to home. He would impersonate the Sultan of Zanzibar, Sayyid Ali ibn Hamud Al-Busaid, during his planned visit to England. Horace would play the role of the

Neville's Court, where Horace de Vere Cole spent his second year. (Jamie Collinson)

sultan for a state visit to Cambridge, a perfect chance to play to a home crowd, and if the plan succeeded it would be all the sweeter that the University authorities had not spotted their own student. However, the prank was not wholly targeted at the University; Cole and his friends correctly surmised that the University was likely to be far more lenient if the hoax was targeted at the mayor. He knew that there was no love lost between town and gown, and that many in the University hierarchy would secretly love to see a joke at the mayor's expense.

The plot was simple and followed the model of several before it, most notably a hoax visit from the 'Shah of Persia' in 1873, which was witnessed by Horace's father. Cole and his friends would dress as the sultan and his entourage and enjoy the hospitality of a welcoming city to a visiting royal. Zanzibar was a good choice as it was a name very much in the national zeitgeist. It was exotic and connoted the romance and mystery of popular stories of the day. At the music hall *The Sultan of Zanzibar* had been playing since the 1880s, and a state visit from the (supposedly) real sultan was bound to draw crowds.

Of course Horace would play the part of the sultan, suitably attired and with skin darkened. Three friends would act as his Zanzibarian suite, similarly made up, though with slightly less impressive costumes. Two of these attendants had studied at Harrow with the English-educated sultan, and thus were well versed in his manners, knew his appearance, and also held an extra motive to carry out the hoax. The sultan had not been popular at school, being well known for trumpeting his status, and had even threatened one older boy that he would cut off his head for the impudence of asking the sultan to run an errand for him. The two from Harrow would be very pleased to have a little fun at his expense. The last member of the party was very important; he would play the part of the translator. Though in reality none would be required as the sultan spoke English perfectly, it was thought that the public would expect a dignitary to speak through an interpreter. Since he would not be in costume a friend from Oxford was chosen, who would not be easily recognisable to the members of the University present.

It was known that the real sultan would be in London on 2 March (1905), offering a perfectly plausible date for him to take a trip up to visit Cambridge. On Wednesday 1 March, Horace travelled to London for the house-warming party of a friend's sisters, Vanessa and Virginia. The sisters in question would feature quite heavily in Cole's life, taking part in his later Dreadnought Hoax, and one would become very famous when she married into the Woolf family. The rest took an early train on Thursday morning, and all met in Covent Garden to be made up by the famous costume artist Willy Clarkson. Clarkson was a strange figure, with a plump body, red face and curled red moustache, but was well respected in theatrical circles and had even supplied clothes and wigs for performances at court, leading Edward VII to appoint him as 'Royal Perruquier and Costumier'.

Clarkson did a wonderful job on the group, who looked very convincing in their stately robes. Horace in particular was very pleased with his appearance, and with full black beard, darkened skin and headscarf was confident that he could fool any petty official. A telegram was sent to the Mayor of Cambridge and signed Henry Lucas, 'simply because someone said that high colonial officials always bore that name':

Reply paid: Strand, Southampton Street

To the Mayor of Cambridge
The Sultan of Zanzibar will arrive today at Cambridge at 4.27 for a short visit. Could you arrange to show him buildings of interest and send carriage?

HENRY LUCAS, Hotel Cecil, London

There was one hitch – as they sent the telegram it was discovered that the real sultan had announced a public visit to the Palace for that afternoon, and along with the stories in the press were plentiful pictures of the sultan. Before they had a chance to change their plans the mayor responded encouragingly – there was no going back, the plan would have to go ahead or be called off for good.

Horace decided to change his character to the sultan's uncle, 'Prince Mukasa Ali' and continue with the visit as planned. One suspects that with the mayor on the hook and already in full costume he could not bear to let the plan go. Photographs of the costumed hoaxers taken before their trip to Cambridge suggest that the others may not have been quite so happy. Looking rather uncomfortable and miserable, they were either carried along by the force of Horace's personality, or perhaps were simply suffering under their make-up. The photographs themselves are remarkable and show Cole's flair for publicity using what was then cutting-edge technology. Without the posed photographs of the hoaxers in full dress it is doubtful that the prank would have caused such a stir or been preserved for posterity.

Attracting large crowds at the station, the troupe took their train journey to Cambridge in relative relaxation. At their destination they were met by the mayor's carriage, which took them to the waiting mayor at the Guildhall. The mayor himself was visibly anxious at meeting such exalted guests, and was no less nervous when told that he would meet the sultan's uncle rather than the sultan himself. Horace had only to grunt and the mayor and town clerk bowed and welcomed the party with civic obsequiousness. One of the hoaxers nearly gave the game away by exclaiming 'Shit!' as he caught his robes on the carriage door. The town dignitaries did not hear, or assumed they had misheard, and the charade went on. After much salaaming the mayor presented Horace with a guidebook to Cambridge and, showing much cultural ignorance, champagne. Horace reciprocated with a portion of 'the dorsal fin from the Sacred Shark of Zanzibar', before following the mayor into a charity bazaar in the Guildhall.

At the bazaar he and his entourage made extravagant purchases while strolling through the stalls. The 'translator' assuring the mayor that the prince was very much enjoying his tour, and that Cambridge clearly had markets which could rival any souq in Africa. A sticky moment occurred when an elderly woman followed the party, claimed that she could speak the prince's native language and asked to have a few words with him. Of course Horace spoke no such tongue, and despite the mayor's pride at one of his residents speaking Zanzibarian, she was quickly discouraged when told that it was only possible for her to talk to the prince if she first entered his harem.

Leaving the Guildhall, Horace and his company were led the short distance to King's College. Enjoying the gathering crowds and now flushed with the early success of the role, he was only slightly concerned that someone might spot the initials 'H de VC' engraved on his umbrella. At King's the party passed a friend, fellow undergraduate Shane Leslie, who was completely taken in by the disguises. Writing in his memoirs, Leslie was full of admiration for the foreigners:

An elderly woman claimed she could speak the Prince's native language.
(Catherine Cox)

The tall swarthy sons of the Prophet in their splendid turbans, their portly tread and the polite gesticulation with which they lifted their arms in mild amazement at all the sights which they were shown, made a lasting picture.

Declining to enter the famous chapel due to their following Islam, the procession snaked towards Trinity, Horace's own college. Here the danger of detection was the greatest, but so too was the thrill of deceit. He could not help but be excited as, entering through the college gate, the porters who he had often clashed with as a student bowed and doffed their hats to him. Exclaiming at the magnificence of the Great Court they played the role of impressed visitors well, but something in the way they moved through the college was suspiciously confident. The town clerk noted to the mayor that, 'these people seem to know their way about', but who would dare challenge a royal party?

After running into several friends, none of whom were any the wiser as to their true identity, Cole began to get bored and the guests expressed their thanks and gave apologies to the mayor that they would have to leave and catch their 7.05 p.m. train back to London. In fact they had no such aim, as the four Cambridge undergraduates would need to be back in their colleges by 10 p.m., leaving no time for a return trip to the City. At the station the city's dignitaries were treated to another theatrical session of salaaming by the prince and his entourage. No sooner had the mayor left the station than the four costumed undergraduates turned and rushed out of the station, leaving their Oxford friend to catch the train back to his University. Hurriedly catching a taxi outside, they retreated to a house on Trumpington Road, leaving a very confused driver wondering who his fares really were.

The next day, now bereft of costume and makeup, Horace travelled to the offices of the *Daily Mail* to offer the details of his hoax for

Prince Mukasa Ali makes his escape. (Catherine Cox)

publication. Cole was always hungry for recognition and showed a remarkable grasp of public relations far advanced of his generation. He knew that by getting the story out first, with the slant he wanted, he could control it. The staff there were initially suspicious, wondering if this was perhaps another hoax at their expense, and sent a reporter back to Cambridge to verify the story. The mayor, still ignorant of the prank, gave an unfortunate interview to the *Mail* telling them that he 'expressed regret at being unable to receive the visitors more fittingly'. The following day the *Mail* broke the story, 'Mayor Hoaxed. Cambridge Undergraduates Daring Trick. Supposed Royal Visit. Imposters Received With Civic Honours.'

The mayor was greatly embarrassed and Horace triumphant. Despite his name being kept out of the papers, everyone in Cambridge soon came to know who was behind the hoax. Horace did little to keep quiet about his role as architect of the prank, and revelled in the attention. Sitting in his 'Zanzibar' rooms, surrounded by exotic fruit and flowers, Horace held court over the crowds of students who would come to visit the famous prankster. Pilgrims to the joker's inner sanctum would receive a copy of the posed pre-prank photograph, signed 'Mukasa Ali, Princeps Zanzibaris'. It was not long before these were in wild circulation, proving popular enough to be copied and sold on the streets as postcards. As hoped, the University did nothing to punish the hoaxers, helped by Horace making sure that the mayor was the butt of the joke in the press. Cole enjoyed a position of celebrity for the rest of his University life, but could not focus on his studies. He failed to sit his final exams and graduated with what he termed a 'First Class, Practical Jokes Degree (Honours)'.

His 'degree' finished and newly wealthy from a large inheritance, Horace took himself on a grand tour of Europe. In Paris he got up to his old tricks and enjoyed the bohemian scene and pranks in equal measure. Amongst playing with the latest motorcars and engaging in duels in the Bois de Boulogne he invented a jape which he would repeat throughout his life. Finding someone to take the wager that he could not lie in the middle of a busy road for an hour, Horace proceeded with a vehicle to the Champs Elysees. There in the middle of the Place de l'Opera he made as if it had broken down and spent the next hour underneath it while the rest of the traffic continued around him. Many thought him implicated with the heist of the Mona Lisa, but he always denied any involvement. For an interview in 1926 with the *Daily Express* he wrote a little poem:

> I never took the Mona Lisa
> Nor the jewels from the castle
> Nor overturned the tower of Pisa
> Nor put the Gold Cup in a parcel

Leaving Paris, he headed for Italy, a country he had long wished to visit. En-route he became mixed up in a local political struggle and was shot in the leg by a fisherman from Corsica. In Venice he became a gondolier, attracting much attention from pretty female tourists and getting into trouble with jealous locals. On the Lido one day he missed death by inches when a bullet fired by a rival flew past his head. Before leaving Venice due to the unwanted attentions of one of his passengers (it is unclear whether the person was male or female), he pulled off another famous prank. It must have been an unpleasant one to carry out, as during the night he quietly sneaked around the Piazzo San Marco, leaving piles of horse manure as he went. The waking city was confused as the Piazzo and the surrounding area can only be reached by boat.

After an unhappy love affair in Rome, Horace returned to London determined to show he still had the guts to carry out a grand hoax. Noting the willingness of the Royal Navy to treat a 1909 Chinese Naval Mission to a full tour of the fleet, Cole entertained a re-interpretation of the Sultan of Zanzibar Joke. He would impersonate the Emperor of Abyssinia and take a tour of HMS *Dreadnought*, flagship of the Home Fleet.

Dreadnought was a daring and politically charged target. Her launch in 1906 was an important point in Britain's pre-war arms race with Germany. At the time the most complex machine in the world, she was a revolutionary battleship, launching a new class of 'dreadnoughts' and rendering previous models obsolete. Unfortunately, such power came at a cost of over £1.5 million (approximately £600 million today) per vessel, and when four more of the new ships were promised in the budget of 1909 it became a huge election issue. The hoax was planned for 7 February 1910, three days before the General Election, and so it seems fair to assume that Horace intended it to be a political statement – why spend such vast sums on warlike posturing when the money could be spent on welfare and reducing taxes?

With the national attention that the hoax would undoubtedly generate came higher stakes. Fooling the Royal Navy would be much more difficult than fooling the Mayor of Cambridge. If caught the consequences could be severe indeed; where before the chief risk was being sent down from the University, now Horace risked being shot or imprisoned. Much more care would have to be taken on the preparations for the hoax, and there would be no opportunity for the kind of quick exit made at the end of the Zanzibar Joke – after all, they would be on-board a battleship!

With this in mind Cole planned carefully, choosing Abyssinia not just for its obscurity in Britain, where few knew anything about the country, but also because it was an important strategic ally in North Africa. Learning from his previous hoax, Horace decided not to impersonate the Emperor himself, but instead an invented cousin 'Ras 'el Makalen'. Even someone who knew something about Abyssinian royalty would be unlikely to question an obscure prince. The costume and make-up would again be entrusted to Willy Clarkson, who made up outfits using a book of patterns which Horace supplied. The end result looked like something straight from the music hall – colourful, flashy and the complete opposite of the simple mode of dress favoured by actual Abyssinians. For this very reason the costumes worked perfectly, as they looked exactly how the British expected an African to dress. Horace had visited North Africa on his grand tour so it is likely he knew this and was playing on the prejudices of the British.

Finding accomplices proved difficult. Many of his friends showed an interest in the scheme but hastily backed out as the reality of the hoax dawned on them. By some accounts even Horace himself became frightened at what he set out to do as it became clear that this was no simple University prank. With less than a week to go, Cole had only two men ready to follow him, one was Adrian Stephen, a lifelong friend and co-conspirator of Zanzibar, the other a mere acquaintance. Fortunately Adrian persuaded another two friends, and with a team of five Horace felt happy the hoax could be achieved. An unexpected event was Adrian's sister Virginia (later Woolf) demanding to join in. At first the men discouraged her, claiming that there was no role for a woman, and that the scheme was simply too dangerous – Horace said to her, 'If we're found out we'll be thrown overboard for certain. They'd pitch us overboard without a thought.' Virginia would not give in, and after much pleading the men gave in. However, they thought a 'princess' in the party would be suspicious, and so Virginia opted to be disguised as a man. As Willy Clarkson recalled:

> Her first make-up was a failure, the project was almost abandoned; but I felt piqued at being thwarted from an effect which I knew could be obtained and made a fresh start. This time the result was astounding in its realism. The beautiful girl had vanished, and in her place was a slim, dignified, dusky nobleman with a sombre countenance and a flowing regal beard.

All was set. Horace and Adrian elected this time to play the roles of British officials. Horace would be 'Mr Herbert Cholmondeley' of the Foreign Office while Adrian would act as the Abyssinians' 'interpreter'. The others would play 'Ras 'el Makalen' and his three family members. Disguises complete, the party visited the Lafayette Studio on Bond Street, and as with Zanzibar took staged photographs for posterity, and the press. After a brief reception at Paddington station, they were in a private railway carriage and speeding towards Weymouth, where *Dreadnought* was docked. Now there was no turning back. In addition to the six hoaxers, Horace had left a seventh man (wonderfully named Tudor Castle) in London. As soon as the

The Abyssinian dignitaries. From left to right, back row: Guy Ridley, Horace de Vere Cole,
Adrian Stephen, Duncan Grant. Front row: Virginia Stephen and Anthony Buxton.
(Private Collection/ The Bridgeman Art Library)

train departed he sent a telegraph to Admiral May, the Commander in
Chief of the Home Fleet:

> To: C in C Home Fleet Portland
> Prince Makalen of Abyssinia and suite arrive 4.20 today Weymouth
> he wishes to see Dreadnought. Kindly arrange meet them on arrival
> regret short notice forgot wire interpreter accompanies them
> Hardinge Foreign Office

So matter-of-fact was the telegram that it was accepted without question, and on arrival at Weymouth station the princes were met by the admiral's flag lieutenant in full uniform. The Royal Navy had bitten, and the hoax was well and truly underway. Taking the steam launch from the quay to the battleship, Horace and Adrian, experienced from Cambridge, settled into their element. They knew that with the party's identity accepted the hard part was over. The princes did not feel so confident, this was new territory for them, and aside from anything, they were starving since they had not eaten a thing since putting their make-up on for fear of smudging it. By strange coincidence, as they boarded *Dreadnought* the band struck up the national anthem of Zanzibar as the bandmaster didn't know the Abyssinian anthem, this must have given Horace a smile in light of the previous hoax.

Stepping on board, they were met by Admiral May and his top staff, resplendent in their medals and dress uniforms. After short introductions, May led the party to the guard of honour for an inspection. Ad-libing, Adrian asked the Admiral about the details on his crew's uniforms, into which May launched with great detail. Things went well with the admiral prattling on about the minutiae of buttons and braiding, until he asked Adrian to translate his answers for the princes. The party had practised a little Swahili on the train, reading from a translated Bible they had brought with them. Adrian began 'Entaqui, mahai, kustafani' but his grasp of the language soon stumbled. Thinking quickly, he switched into Latin and Classical Greek, using verses remembered from school and quoting the Aeneid. By mispronouncing words and avoiding well-known Latin phrases the officers were fooled – their education had not been as expensive as the pranksters.

Having inspected the guard, they were invited to take tea in the wardroom. Playing a Foreign Office mandarin, Horace readily accepted, but Adrian declined on behalf of the princes as he knew their disguises would not stand up to eating or drinking. He explained that for religious reasons their food had to be specially prepared, adding detail to the tale he went on to mention that as Muslims they would perform the prostrate prayer ceremony on the deck at sunset. A mistake as each prince wore an obvious crucifix, and Abyssinia was a predominantly Christian country. Though no one noticed this inconsistency the Admiral was not pleased at the idea of a Muslim ritual being carried out on a Royal Navy ship. In consequence he officially delayed sunset across the fleet, in order that the princes could leave before they had to pray. Next the party took a tour of the ship's impressive guns, though the offer of them firing a royal salute was politely declined. Then a real problem occurred, as the weather changed and a light rain began. As beards began to peel away and make-up run, Adrian hurriedly told the ship's captain how cold the climate was compared to the princes' native country, and they were quickly taken below deck for a tour of the wireless room.

On meeting up with Horace again all decided it was time to leave. They had a train to catch and there was nothing they could do further to make the hoax more successful for it had already exceeded expectations. They returned from *Dreadnought* as they had arrived, on the steam launch and accompanied by the flag lieutenant. The lieutenant had been told at length by Horace about the princes' many wives and spent the journey asking about the practicality of such an arrangement. At the station they caught the train without incident and left the Navy convinced that they had received an authentic royal visit. There was only one problem – it had all gone too well and the officers had been so kind that all felt rather guilty. Horace had never intended to mock the men; his target was the ship and politicians who had commissioned her. As a result, all agreed that they would not go to the press, and the affair would remain a private joke.

Unfortunately, Horace was not good at keeping a joke private. Returning to London, he could not help but mention the hoax to friends at his club, one of whom was so troubled with the ease at which strangers could get on board the Navy's flagship that he informed the Foreign Office. Horace went to Whitehall to confess but no one believed him. However, news of the event reached the Admiralty, who began an investigation. One suspects that they would have been happy to suppress the story, but four days later, on Saturday 12 February, the story hit the front page of the *Express*, 'Sham Abyssinian Princes visit the Dreadnought'. The Navy was shamed, and so was Admiral May. The public went wild with the story and it was not long before the identity of the hoaxers leaked out. Horace was now famous on a national level and the hoax started a new trend for costume parties. Fancy-dress shops in London had never seen so much business. The music halls took up the hoax as a favourite subject, one ditty from the time was:

> When I went on board a Dreadnought ship
> I looked like a costermonger;
> They said I was an Abyssinian prince
> 'Cos I shouted 'Bunga Bunga!'

This cry of 'bunga bunga' had never been used by the hoaxers, it had been invented by the *Express* in its articles, but soon became a signature of the hoax and for years after children would shout it in the street to passing sailors. The officers of the *Dreadnought* were not pleased by the mocking, and sought out Horace for revenge. In a strange incident two sailors visited Cole, demanding that he re-enact the hoax before apologising to the Admiral. Declining this, Horace offered to meet either officer 'with boxing-gloves, sword or revolver' to settle the matter. Not liking this idea, the sailors suggested a caning. Cole jokingly agreed on the condition that he be allowed to cane the officer back. Surprisingly they agreed and, retiring to a nearby alley, Horace gave six strokes of the cane to the officer, before receiving six strokes in return. Satisfied, the officers left and Cole was never bothered by the Navy again.

Unfortunately this was Horace's zenith. His great hoax was featured on the stage and silver screen (in a silent film *Sealed Orders* in 1918), but he began to fade. Nevertheless, he continued to play minor but notable pranks. A friend, Oliver Locker-Lampson, became an MP and boasted that as such he could not be tried for a criminal offence (other accounts state that he was espousing the opinion that 'an innocent man has nothing to fear from the law'). To test this, Horace slipped his pocket watch into Oliver's pocket and challenged him to a race down the street. The young MP bolted off and Horace shouted 'Stop! Thief!' and Locker-Lampson had a sticky conversation with a policeman.

Another was Cole's personal favourite. He would dress as a surveyor with clipboard and string, and stand in Piccadilly. There he would find a well-dressed man with 'bowler hat and rolled umbrella' and ask the victim to hold one end of the string while he measured something. When the good citizen politely obliged he would retreat round the corner, find another willing victim, and hand them the other end of the string. At this point Cole would retire to a pub or café with good views of the location and watch the ensuing altercation.

Piccadilly was a favourite haunt and the location of another post-*Dreadnought* prank. Once again using the skills of Willy Clarkson, Horace and friends dressed as navvies, complete with tools, rope and road-signs. Heading to the Cavalry Club at 127 Piccadilly, Cole recruited a witless policeman to redirect traffic while he set about digging up the road. After half an hour a large hole had been produced, and the crew of 'workmen' disappeared to watch the resulting chaos.

According to the *Oxford Dictionary of National Biography*, to show his dislike for a certain play, Horace 'gave tickets to a large number of bald men whose pates seen from the dress circle spelt out an expletive; characteristically he even remembered to dot the "i".'

But Horace could not live up to his public persona. He was growing older and seemed to be stuck in a generation which had passed. With the rise of the absurd and surreal comedy of the Modernists he now seemed passé and old-fashioned. He tried to change his style, away from the large scale pre-planned pranks of his youth, and into spontaneous, visceral performances. Examples are rare, but those recorded include Horace feigning a fit in a crowded ballroom. Thinking him dying, the last rites were administered before he sprang back into life. In another he went to sleep in a bed in the window of a furniture store. In yet another he walked off a station platform in front of a stopping train to light his cigar off the engine, narrowly missing death beneath its wheels. One which observers would certainly never forget was his 'cow's teat' prank. Walking down the street with a cow's teat sticking out of his trouser flies, Horace would walk up to a policeman, wait for a crowd to form as he was told to cover up his indecent display, and then pull out a knife and cut the teat off.

As the years passed, his life spiralled unhappily downwards. His money lost in bad investments and partners driven away by his strange moods, Horace eventually found a kind of peace in a modest cottage in Normandy near Honfleur. There passed away the greatest of all hoaxers.

THE WATER VELOCIPEDE

Horace de Vere Cole may have been the greatest of all hoaxers, but he was certainly not the first, nor is he likely to be the last. One of the earliest known Cambridge hoaxes occurred on 29 May 1822, when posters appeared all over town stating:

> Zachariah Whitmore of Philadelphia, North America, begs to inform the inhabitants of Cambridge that he intends starting from Lynn on his Water Velocipede at 12 o'clock, and will arrive at Cambridge between 6 and 7 o'clock in the evening on Whit Monday next!

One wonders what people imagined this water velocipede to look like (designs vary from tricycles with inflatable balloon wheels to canoes with paddle-wheels), but whatever they expected the townsfolk were anxious to see it and turned out in droves. Local papers reported afterwards that over 2,000 people waited at the riverside for several hours before realising they had been hoaxed. This was a significant number given that the city's population according to the 1821 census was only 14,142.

THE SHAH OF PERSIA

A direct influence on Cole was an earlier hoax of 1873, delightfully reported in the *New York Times* as 'An Able Practical Joke, It Created Much Excitement in a University City'. At the time Britain was awash with talk about the visit of the Shah of Persia, dressed 'in an astrakhan cap and a long coat embroidered with gold and wearing as many diamonds and precious stones as his apparel would bear,' he cut an exotic figure and fascinated the people of England. 'Have you seen the Shah?' became a popular catchphrase on the street and in the music-halls.

This interest was taken advantage of by one mischievous student, and at 11 a.m. on Saturday, 28 June 1873 a telegram arrived at the Guildhall in Cambridge. It was directed to the Worshipful Mayor of Cambridge, was signed by one Lieut. Col. Hamilton, and read:

> His Imperial Majesty, the Shah of Persia desires to visit your University town to-day, en-route for London by special, arriving at Cambridge Station about 1:10 o'clock. Be prepared with escort and reception as far as time will allow.

Instantly the civic machine sprang into action. The town clerk was sent for, and messages were dispatched to the Vice Chancellor of the University, the members of the Town Corporation and the cook of Peterhouse. The Vice Chancellor and councillors hurried into their robes, others donned their uniforms, and the cook began to prepare a banquet. The public were informed and hung out banners in the street, where large crowds gathered to catch a glimpse of the Shah. The dignitaries hurried to the station as fast as their dignity would allow, and met with an honour guard and carriages which had been prepared. The only one missing was the Shah. As quickly as the visit had arrived, it collapsed. News got around that the railway officials knew nothing about a special train, and it was soon apparent that the whole thing was a hoax. The general public minded very little, having got their entertainment from the flustered bigwigs. A few days after the 'visit' song sheets were sold in the streets and proved to be very popular. Part of the verse read:

> The Mayor and Council so queer did look,
> As from the station they took their hook;
> The Chancellor the back slums did go,
> As he didn't want all the people to know,
> That he didn't see the Shah of Persia.

HADDOCK'S SPEECH

In 1909 another hoax which may have influenced Cole's political stunts was perpetrated in the hall of Emmanuel College. A talented member of the University Amateur Dramatic Club, Mr W.M. Malleson, impersonated a liberal Conservative MP from Liverpool, a Mr G.B. Haddock. Disguised with grey moustache and beard and made-up by Horace de Vere Cole's friend Willy Clarkson, he delivered a pithy address opposing Women's Suffrage. The hoax was described by one local paper as one of the most successful ever carried out: 'From first to last, despite the name of "Haddock" there was no suspicion of "cod" on the part of the audience who took the debate in real earnest.'

THE POST-IMPRESSIONIST EXHIBITION

In 1913 a truly great hoax was carried out by a small group of Cambridge students. Somewhat unusually, the focus of this hoax was not making fun of the establishment, but attacking a new art movement which offended traditional sensibilities. In 1910, Roger Fry had organised an exhibition titled' Manet and the Post-Impressionists' (a term which he had invented), which served to introduce the British public to the work of Manet, Matisse, Gaugin and Van Gogh. This was soon followed by his Second Post-Impressionist Exhibition in 1912. Many were baffled by the work – British art critics were still digesting the Impressionism of Monet and Renoir, and found Post-Impressionism simply too avant-garde. Some even thought Fry's exhibitions were themselves hoaxes. However, the movement did have its fans, and small Post-Impressionist exhibitions occurred throughout the country. After one such exhibition took place in Cambridge a group from the Natural Sciences Club decided to put on a Post-Impressionist exhibition of their own, and theirs most certainly would be a hoax.

The chief architect of the plan was Archibald Don, a student of Natural Sciences at Trinity College who had stayed on after his graduation in 1912 to obtain the qualifications necessary to become a doctor of medicine. He was accompanied by his friend, E.D. Adrian, later Lord Adrian, who would come to serve as Master of Trinity from 1951-65, and Chancellor of the University from 1967-75. Adrian gave a full account of the origins of the exhibition:

> There is in Cambridge a time-honoured institution called the Natural Sciences Club. The members were all undergraduates or B.A.'s, and although the number of in residence was seldom above fifteen, the club boasted of a long list of Fellows of the Royal Society amongst its past members. At each meeting a paper would be read on a matter of scientific interest, and a technical discussion would follow. After this the talk would drift into every conceivable topic. The meeting which gave birth to the Expressionist Exhibition was held in Don's rooms in the Great Court of Trinity. We began to talk about the pictures at the Grafton Gallery, which Don had been to see a day or two before. He was very angry with the whole school, with their laboured crudity and their wilful neglect of all that had been won for them by past generations of artists. He drew little sketches on odd bits of paper to illustrate his point, and soon we were all infected by his talk and imitating Matisse and Picasso. Judging from the results of these efforts, it appeared that the less one knew

of drawing the more likely one would be to produce a picture with the true post-impressionist spirit.

Don did not give up on this idea, and the next day he proposed an exhibition to 'show the absurdity of neglecting good craftsmanship for the sake of theatrical simplicity.' With Don's infectious enthusiasm, he soon had a group of eight or nine friends buying unfamiliar brushes, tubes of paint, and oils and turpentine. With this manpower an exhibition of works could really go ahead. Don intended it to be a serious attempt at criticism, to show that crudity and ugliness are not necessarily the product of an inspired artist, but may simply result from someone who is unable to produce finesse and beauty. Despite their lofty goals, it was not long before the pictures produced took their inspiration from friends, enemies and University jokes. Another stumbling block was that several pieces produced held genuine merit. Adrian recalls that Don's first piece, a portrait in the style of Picasso, was 'so true to its subject that it was really a strong argument in favour of instead of against the post-impressionist school.'

It is a measure of Don's motivating powers how quickly a body of work was assembled. The meeting of the Cambridge University Natural Sciences Club which Adrian mentioned was held on Saturday 15 February. Once they were sure sufficient pictures could be produced a small room at the Guildhall was booked for a week, beginning Tuesday 4 March, and by the end of the month the pranksters had prepared posters to advertise their exhibition and had begun to announce it to the press. Don managed to plant a letter advertising the exhibition in the *Cambridge Magazine* on 1 March:

> The Cambridge Magazine has shown itself so broadmindedly interested in what has come to be known, somewhat unfortunately, as Post Impressionism, that we venture to call your attention to an exhibition of Pictures and Studies to be held in the Guildhall next week. We do not for one moment pretend to have reached the stage of technical skill which was so conspicuously displayed in

most, though perhaps not all, of those wonderful pictures at the Grafton. We are full of hope that our attempts, however far they may fall short of the ideal, will enable at least a few in Cambridge to appreciate more fully that group of much abused masters who are struggling so valiantly against an incredible mass of prejudice in their effort to sever the cords which bind photography and art so miserably together.

The conspirators' *pièce de résistance* was the catalogue of works itself. The front cover adorned with a reduced version of their poster for the exhibition, the introduction was unsigned but credited to 'a sympathetic, but discriminating friend'. It was in fact written by none other than (Sir) Walter Lamb, later Secretary of the Royal Academy of Arts (1913-51) and brother of the painter Henry Lamb, whose works would feature in the Post-Impressionism exhibition held at the Royal Academy in 1979-80. Lamb wrote several cryptic descriptions of individual works – e.g. 'The simplification in this picture might be carried even further, without loss of significance', or 'Very plastic', or 'The colouring is suggestively stertorous'. However, it is his introduction which is most memorable:

'Unsophisticated' is the epithet which best describes the outstanding quality of the works in the present exhibition; unless, encouraged by their inventive daring, one should make a new word, and say 'antisophistic'. For these artists, on their part, have been encouraged by Post Impressionism to utter their discontent in one of the chief strongholds of academic culture. They have learnt that the sin of art, as of all that affects the upper life of the mind, is science. They have thrown away the tools which their fathers patented.

In all, Don assembled a collection of eighty-six pictures to show at the exhibition, which was to be titled 'Seven Cambridge Expressionists'. The seven were actually twelve in total, eleven from Cambridge and one rather special guest. Though the public catalogue kept each of the artists anonymous, Adrian and Don each kept their own copy, identifying the painter and (if sold) buyer of each piece. The eleven students produced eighty-five of the pictures, with Don predictably the most prolific having produced twenty-four of the works. Adrian managed a respectable seventeen, with their friends producing the remainder. The eighty-sixth was contributed by the painter Sir Philip Burne-Jones (1861–1926). Don wrote to tell him about the exhibition, knowing how little he cared for the post-impressionists. Burne-Jones responded on 3 March:

> I at once set to work, and painted a Post-Impressionist picture for the Show. I call it 'Fame'. Any other name would do as well – 'Maternite', 'Eclos du temps passe' – 'Anaesthesia' – 'A Morning Walk' – anything. I happen to call it 'Fame'. It will reach you, carriage paid, ready framed, and under glass – (because the paint isn't at all dry, as it was only put on today!) – tomorrow afternoon. May it have a humble place on your walls? 'Gustave Duclos' would do as well as any other name for the painter.

The day before the opening on Tuesday 4 March, there was a private viewing of the collection for the press. The art critic for the *Morning Post*, James Greig, came down from London and was shown the collection by Don and Adrian. Adrian guessed that Greig had not been fooled by the hoax, recalling 'He must have seen at once that the aims of the exhibitors were not as serious as their catalogue suggested. However, he gave no hint of this … [and] played his part so well that for some hours afterwards Don was not sure whether he had taken it seriously or not.' Don wrote a note to his mother, 'So busy. But must just send line. Everything going splendid. The Morning Post critic came down today and SWALLOWED THE WHOLE SHOW. At least unless he was acting as well as me – he was quite taken in!'

The following morning Greig's review appeared, and proved that he was not as naive as Don had thought. He began by taking much relish in how he had observed true believers in the post-impressionist movement taken in by a spoof exhibition staged by members of the

The Cambridge Post-Impressionist Exhibition. (Catherine Cox)

Chelsea Arts Club, then railed against the movement as a whole. He continued:

> A few undergraduates of Cambridge have arranged a similar exhibition, which will open from today until the end of the week in a small room at the Guildhall. There were eighty pictures and drawings, the work of 'Seven Cambridge Expressionists'. Their names were kept secret, but we had the good fortune to see several of the artists. They were absolutely unlike the professional types we have referred to. All were fine, strapping fellows who could row in a Varsity eight quite as well as they can paint. Of course, their pictures are in the manner of the Cubists and their kind, but several of them have the freshness of colour if not of idea that is pleasant to the eye. The point to be noted is that the success of these Cambridge amateurs proves how easy are the methods of the artists they imitate, that it is within the power of almost anyone to be a Post-Impressionist. A lack of conscience seems to be the chief essential.

In spite of Greig's revealing review, the exhibition continued with many visitors being completely taken in. After two days Don wrote to his mother to tell her that the exhibition had so far made £15 (about £1,000 in today's money). Adrian wrote that several visitors 'were sufficiently enlightened to buy some of the pictures as genuine examples of the post-impressionist school'. A review by A.C. Piggott of Pembroke College, published in the *Cambridge Chronicle* on 6 March, suggests that not all of the critics got the joke either, writing 'The seven expressionists who are exhibiting at the Guildhall, Cambridge, are neither better nor worse than other exploiters of Post-Impressionism. The crudity of their colouring is as tiring to the eye as the crudity of their symbolism is painful to the imagination.' A further negative review was placed in the *Cambridge Review* on 6 March, though on closer inspection was written by one Adrian Robertson – a combination of Adrian and Don's names – and was clearly intended to stoke the fire of publicity further.

When the exhibition closed on Saturday 8 March, the conspirators felt they had enjoyed much success, and celebrated with a dinner given in honour of Don. In total they had sold twenty of their paintings, entertained more than 1,000 visitors, taken a total of £55 (about £3,500 today) and caused a great deal of controversy. Amusingly enough, Sir Philip Burne-Jones' piece was not sold, nor was it appreciated by critics who said it 'lacked the spontaneity and abandon' of the less able undergraduate painters. It was returned to the artist and safely received on 11 March. Of the other pictures some met better fates than others. K.O. Neuman's 'Study for the Councillor' was bought by Mrs Don and used as a wrapper for several others she had purchased. 'Dinner in Hall' fared better and was purchased by Trinity College and hung in the Gallery in the Hall for some time before disappearing from sight. Mansfield Forbes' 'Bataille Maritime d'Egypt' was purchased for one and a half guineas, subsequently given to Lord Adrian and inherited by his son, and now hangs in the study of the Master's Lodge at Pembroke.

Aptly, the most interesting survivor is Don's 'The Velvet Glove'. Described as a 'not altogether unrecognisable portrait', the work is a Picasso-inspired caricature of the then Master of Trinity, Montagu Butler. Butler was a well-known public figure and had twice been caricatured in *Vanity Fair*. He was famous both for his skull-cap and for wearing mittens in chapel to keep warm. Don's work is a geometric chaos featuring a skull-capped face with a crude mitten held in front of its mouth. If this was not enough, to suggest the subject, the painting includes heavy symbolism in the form of the letters 'TRI', the numbers '3' and 'III' and many three-pointed stars, clovers and other geometric shapes. 'The Velvet Glove' was purchased by Don's mother at the exhibition and she subsequently gave the painting to Adrian in 1919. He accepted it on behalf of the college and upon Adrian becoming Master of Trinity, it was given a position in his rooms in the Master's Lodge. It was returned there after Adrian's death and now hangs, discreetly, above the stairs beyond the Great Drawing Room.

THE VISIT OF SIR ARTHUR CONAN DOYLE

A hoax of 1921 saw Cambridge awaiting the famous author of the *Sherlock Holmes* novels. Conan Doyle was a well-known member of the Spiritualist movement, notably writing a book on the Cottingley Fairy photographs which he was convinced were real. This lent credibility to the posters put up around the city announcing that Sir Arthur Conan Doyle would be presenting a lecture in the Guildhall on 'Sex Equality After Death'. The posters went on to explain that Conan Doyle would completely prove the theory of materialisation – that the spirits of the dead could exhibit physical form.

As one might expect, the Guildhall was packed with townspeople wanting a glimpse of the famous man. They were shocked, and soon realised they had been hoaxed, when a student clad in ghostly white robes appeared on the stage with a banner reading 'Sir Arthur Conan Doyle Has Failed To Materialise.'

H. ROCHESTER SNEATH

H. Rochester Sneath MA was born in 1900, and in 1948 served as the headmaster to Selhurst School near Petworth, Sussex. Selhurst was a minor public school with around 175 male students. Sneath was something of a strange character who wrote many bizarre letters to public figures, especially other headmasters. This might seem like nothing more than a small slice of upper middle-class British life, but there was one problem. Neither Sneath nor Selhurst existed. Both were inventions of Humphry Berkeley, then an undergraduate at Pembroke College, who enjoyed his alter ego immensely.

In order that the fictitious school should not sound so, Berkeley spent some time testing out possibilities with his new acquaintances at Pembroke. He would steer any conversation towards discussing what his new friends had done prior to Cambridge. After stating their school each would inevitably ask where he had studied, 'Well, as a matter of fact, I was at a school called Selhurst,' would come the reply. When this was met with a blank stare he would continue, 'Haven't you heard of Selhurst?' This was the acid test. With the name Selhurst each undergraduate wilfully lied to cover his perceived ignorance and respond, 'Of course I've heard of it, dear boy.' Berkeley knew he had a winner. With some school letter headings printed up and an arrangement with the Post Office to forward any letter to Selhurst to a friend's address in Cambridge all was set.

In early 1948 Sneath began to send letters to his fellow headmasters – particularly those of prestigious public schools. He began with a short note to the Master of Marlborough College, asking how the college had managed to 'engineer' a visit from the King and Queen. The Master, F.M. Heywood, was certainly not pleased with this wording, and sent back a curt message that the visit had been requested by the King's Private Secretary, and he had simply obliged. Sneath wrote again to Heywood, informing him that a prior employee of Selhurst, the French Master Mr Robert Agincourt, intended to apply for a position at Marlborough. Sneath counselled that in no circumstances should Agincourt be employed, as amongst other things he had climbed a tree in the school grounds naked, and had thrown a flower pot at the wife of the chairman of the school's board of governors. Heywood replied with a single line, still clearly believing Sneath to be a real but eccentric colleague, 'The man whom you have mentioned has not made any approach to me and I require no further information about him.' Finally Sneath pushed Heywood too far, asking to be recommended a private detective and competent nursery maid. Heywood cut off their correspondence, replying, 'I cannot imagine why you should suppose that I employ a private detective, and I am not an agency for domestic servants. I really must ask that you not bother me with this kind of thing.'

The headmaster of Rugby was given some friendly advice: 'Do not be taken in by the hysterical outcries against homosexuality which from time to time appear in the press. I have found that most homosexuality amongst schoolboys is harmless, and you can afford to ignore what is in most cases a purely transitory phase.' The headmaster of Stowe was asked for some advice on sex education as, 'The writings upon the walls of the School lavatories made a visiting Bishop shudder'. While the headmaster of Eton was surprised to hear from Sneath regarding his candidacy as the next Master. Of numerous serious replies from headmasters the prize must go to H.C.A. Gaunt, the Master of Malvern College. Gaunt was so taken in by Sneath's letters that he recommended Selhurst to a friend who was seeking a good school for her son. She wrote a letter of interest to Sneath, who responded that the school had, 'a waiting list which is full until 1962' but that her son could be placed, 'upon our waiting list for the Waiting List'.

Sneath wrote to George Bernard Shaw requesting that he speak at Selhurst's tricentenary celebrations – he declined. Sir William Reid Dick was asked if he might be commissioned to create a statue of the school's founder, Ebenezer Okeshot – Sir William was interested and asked for more details. A letter to Sir Giles Gilbert Scott enquired if he would draw up a design for an expansion to the school named Sneath House – Scott replied that he was busy rebuilding the House of Commons, but otherwise would have been favourable to the idea. Sir Adrian Boult was invited to conduct the first public performance of the Selhurst Symphony – he was already booked up for the date requested. The manager of the Albert Hall was contacted to probe the possibility of holding a rally of Old Selhurstians there – the manager seemed confused as to whether the school would need the capacity of 5,000 people.

Only two recipients caught on to the hoax, and both were imaginative enough to respond in the absurd style of Sneath's letters. The headmaster of Wimbledon College, Revd John Sinnott, responded favourably to Sneath's request to exorcise a ghost, which he believed to be the spirit of a matron who had committed suicide after being seduced by a housemaster. Sinnott replied wryly that he would need 'the usual Bell, Book and Candle, a gallon of holy water and a packet of salt'. He also mentioned that in order to succeed all present (excepting himself) should fast for at least twenty-four hours prior to the ceremony. Walter Oakeshot, headmaster of Winchester, also saw through the prank. He was informed that as a descendent of Ebenezer Okeshot the school would be honoured if he would come to unveil a new plaque commemorating his ancestor. A letter was returned from his private secretary, informing Sneath that sadly the headmaster was overseas visiting Ebenezer Okeshot's grave in Utah, where, as he would no doubt be aware, Okeshot had been killed after an argument with the Pilgrim Mothers.

The hoax might have continued for some time had Sneath not written to a newspaper. His letter, printed in the *Daily Worker* on the difficulty of obtaining Russian textbooks for the compulsory study of Russian at Selhurst, caused quite a stir in the communist-fearing climate of 1948. Although a fine example of his letters (ending, 'English is taught in every Russian school; ought we not to grasp this hand of friendship?'), this would prove to be the end of Sneath. *News Review* attempted to contact the headmaster for an interview on his position. His replies dodged the issue of a face-to-face or telephone interview, and when the reporter took a second look at the name of Sneath's secretary, 'Penelope Pox-Rhyddene', he smelled a rat. Travelling to Petworth the reporter discovered that there was no Selhurst School there. After contacting the major universities and several government offices, no trace of Rochester Sneath could be found either.

Eventually *News Review* caught up with Berkeley via the friend's address he had used to receive many of Sneath's letters. An article revealing the hoax was published and a torrent of headmagisterial letters forced Sir Montagu Butler, the Master of Pembroke College, to send Berkeley down (exile him from the college) for two years. Berkeley thought he saw a twinkle in Butler's eye when he was punished, and noted a warmth on his return, suggesting that Sir Montagu definitely saw the joke.

Berkeley went on to great things. Sir Montagu Butler's son, R.A. Butler (nicknamed Rab), got him a job at Conservative Central Office. It was also Rab who advised Berkeley to keep the Sneath letters secret, and not to publish them for at least twenty-five years. Berkeley became

Conservative MP for Lancaster in 1959, but lost his seat in 1966 after a controversial bill he introduced to legalize homosexual relations. In 1968 he resigned from the Conservative Party over its stance on the Vietnam War, and in 1974 stood unsuccessfully as a Labour candidate. A quarter of a century up, this year also saw the publication of the Rochester Sneath letters as a volume with comic illustrations by Nicolas Bentley. Pre-dating the more famous Henry Root Letters, many believe that Sneath and Selhurst served as inspiration to William Donaldson – who incidentally was also a Cambridge man.

THE SHROVE TUESDAY PANCAKE RACE

The Shrove Tuesday Pancake Race was an amusing hoax about which there is little detail remaining. However, it paints a charming enough image that what little we do know is sufficient. It was apparently publicised and arranged by the Pitt Club, who caused enough publicity to gather several hundred undergraduates on Shrove Tuesday of 1957 to watch the inaugural pancake race between college porters of several colleges. Although the race was soon discovered to be a hoax, a cook working in the Magdalene kitchens, Horace Reed, appeared on the bridge clutching a frying pan and ran the race accompanied by the cheering students.

The Shrove Tuesday Pancake Race.
(Catherine Cox)

Magdalene kitchens, site of the Shrove Tuesday pancake race. (Jamie Collinson)

CANDID CAMERA

In his obituary, the *Independent* described *Candid Camera*'s Jonathon Routh as the 'forefunner to Jeremy Beadle', I would prefer to paint him as more of a follower in the footsteps of Horace de Vere Cole. Like Cole, he came from a venerable family – his father was a British Army colonel, and he could trace the family's origins back to one of William the Conqueror's knights. Also like Cole, his pranks began at an early age and seemed to be directed against unworthy authority and bureaucracy. He won a scholarship to the prestigious Uppingham School but was ejected after hanging a banner reading 'Vote Routh, Communist' in the school chapel.

At Cambridge he read history at Emmanuel College and at first seemed to thrive. Within the first year he had begun editing the student magazine *Granta* and was credited with reviving the Footlights dramatic society. However, at Cambridge he is best remembered for an elaborate prank, much in the mould of Cole, in which he first took a group of students to 'measure' Bletchley for a bypass. They dressed as planners from the highway agency and took copious notes on the area, while announcing to interested locals that the planned motorway bypass would necessitate the bulldozing of Bletchley Park, and ministers had already provisionally approved this. A short while later, he returned to scenes of indignation in Bletchley and began collecting hundreds of signatures against his imaginary bypass, before presenting them to a very confused and harangued local MP.

There is a divergence in opinion as to whether this caused Routh to give up his degree after just one year (it's certainly feasible this was taken as 'bringing the University into disrepute'), or whether he left for personal reasons. A move into journalism followed, and his love of hoaxes which had begun at Cambridge continued. One notable example was the invention of a fictitious eighteenth-century poet, leading to mentions in the *Times Literary Supplement* and in a talk on the BBC *Third Programme*. Another was his arrest after trying, in a taxi,

Measuring Bletchley for a bypass. (Catherine Cox)

to transport a large case inside which lay a man groaning. He was well known for taking a grand piano on the tube, daily leaving a pair of shoes in Kensington public library, and sending himself through the post to Wandsworth covered in postage stamps.

Deciding to turn professional, he put an advert in *The Times*: 'Practical joker with wide experience of British public's sad gullibility organises, leads and guarantees success of large-scale hoaxes.' This led to his starring role in the UK import of *Candid Camera*, a US show with a peculiarly British view on practical jokes. Among many mundane jokes perhaps the best remembered was in his first episode. A car was led down a gentle hill and into a garage, where the mechanic was asked to change the oil. Opening the bonnet he discovered there was no engine, and was filmed looking for it in the boot, under the chassis and even in the back seats.

Routh seemed to particularly enjoy seeing the reactions of those he tricked, and shared Cole's delight at the peculiar way the British dealt with foreigners. Writing in the *Independent* in 2003, Miles Kingston described his trip with Routh on a *Punch* magazine staff outing to Margate. Routh insisted that everyone should visit the home of then Prime Minister Edward Heath's parents: 'We should', he said, 'pretend we were a coachload of French tourists who had come for that sole purpose, and make inquiries for their whereabouts at Broadstairs Tourist Office'. Kingston wrote:

'I will take someone with me, preferably a French-speaker,' said Routh. I volunteered. 'Leave all the talking to me, Miles,' said Routh. 'Pretend you don't understand any English. Talk to me in French if you like. I shall talk to them in English with a heavy French accent. But listen carefully. After a few sentences I will talk to them in plain English without an accent, and they will never notice. They never do.'

'Yes, sir,' said the polite tourist official, when we got to the counter.

'We are a group of French tourists who 'ave come to visit ze 'ouse of ze parents of Monsieur 'Eass, your Prime Minister. Please, where ees eet?'

'Oh, good God,' said the man, sotto voce and looking a bit faint. 'Brian, can you come and help? There's a bus-load of French tourists who … It's not open to the public, monsieur!'

'No matter,' said Routh. 'We will just have a look. And have our photographs taken.'

'Oh no, you can't … they might not like that, you see, it's a private house … Brian! Can you come and help?'

As the conversation progressed, Jonathan got less and less French, and more and more English, until he had reverted to his normal speech. Neither Brian nor the other official noticed that he was no longer French – they talked loudly, and slowly, and heatedly, and addressed him as 'Monsieur', until he went away.

It's not clear whether Routh knowingly took inspiration from Cole's Zanzibar hoax, but Cole would certainly have appreciated it and been envious of Routh's popularity as a public prankster. Routh managed the kind of balance Cole never did, remaining a popular figure and spending the latter part of his life writing and painting. Had Cole been born into the television generation, perhaps he too could have kept hold of public acceptance.

MAGNUS ILLOTUS

Author Brian Clegg recalled a grand hoax he took part in while studying at Selwyn College. The hoax took the form of a fake ceremony, and his account is amongst the most complete of several fractional tales of the same ceremony. It seems to have taken place over the course of several years, but he participated in the events of 9 June 1974 as a member of the choir.

It was a totally fictional ancient ceremony, variously called 'The Immersion of the High Professor' or 'Magnus Illotus' (literally 'great unwashed') and seems to have mostly been aimed at fooling the crowds of tourists evident in the city during the summer. Unlike most student hoaxes, the participants seem to have taken pleasure not in revealing their hoax to the world, but in being part of a small group who knew that the general public had been fooled. Leaflets were handed out to the watching crowds with a little 'history' of the ceremony:

> The first High Professor, Master Ralph de Pittinger, bathed in the River Granta in 1426 to set an example of personal hygiene to his students. Ten years later, his successor, Master Swain Fitz-Dyer, drowned in his 73rd year whilst re-enacting the same ceremony. It was subsequently decreed by the Bull 'Magnus Illotus' of the Anti-Pope Anicletus III that every 73rd Trinity Sunday thereafter, a solemn commemoration of the event be made.

The ceremony featured a procession of hundreds of academics in full dress robes through the centre of the city down King's Parade. The procession was not austere, ambling more than marching through the streets, as Clegg noted, 'we were instructed not to be formal.' For this the police stopped the traffic – an indication of just how extensively planned the hoax was. The procession then entered Trinity College and made its way to the river. Here the don chosen to play the role of the high professor was stripped down to his underwear behind a curtain of cloaks, while a Latin ceremonial was chanted. The choir responded with a further chant, Clegg remembers one couplet was:

> *In combinationibus stat,* (He stands in his combinations)
> *Sancta Michaelis designatus est.* (Labelled 'St Michaels')

The high professor was then slapped across the face with a fish (the handout noted that this part of the ceremony was introduced a few hundred years ago, and that though no one knew why it was performed, it was considered essential), then dipped into the river while the choir sang Superflumina Babyloniis. The ceremony complete, the high professor was then wrapped in a sheet and rowed off down the river. For those who question why anyone would go to all this trouble for a silly prank, Clegg has a telling message:

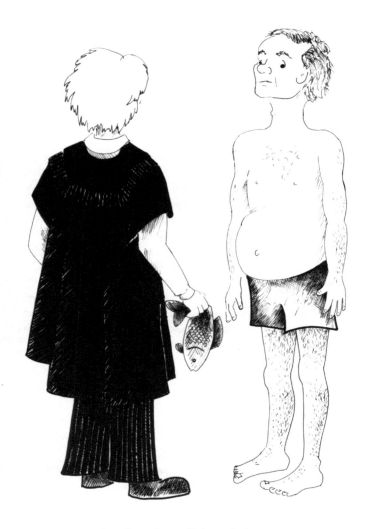

In combinationibus stat. (Catherine Cox)

The best bit of all came about ten years later, at least 100 miles from Cambridge, when we had some people we hadn't seen for ages round for dinner, and one of them told the story of this amazing ceremony he had seen while visiting Cambridge as a tourist – he had been one of the huge audience that assumed it was for real.

THE PEMBROKE TREE

Pembroke is a beautiful college, and the third oldest in Cambridge. Much pride is held in the original buildings surrounding the Old Court (also known as the First Court), including the gatehouse which dates from the fourteenth century and is the oldest in the city. The college is properly called the Hall of Valence Mary, taking its name from the foundress Marie Aylmer de Valence de St Pol de Chastillon. The Old Court was the scene of an amusing prank, which though not strictly a hoax seemed to fit best here.

During the early 1980s, a large tree was planted in the centre of the Old Court lawn, a decision which the student body took offence to, thinking that it spoilt the appearance of the court. Some students removed it. It was replaced by the college, so they removed it again, and it was again replaced by the college. When the students removed the tree a third time the college lost patience and an official notice was issued about the events:

The walnut tree in first court.
The tree which has again been planted in First Court was presented by three fellows to mark a long period of membership of the college and their affection for it.

It will be well known that it was twice uprooted last term, no doubt in good, though misplaced, humour.

It was replanted again at the end of last term and again uprooted at once. This third incident has taken the matter beyond a joke. It can now only be seen as an act of petty vandalism of which I would expect a member of the College to feel ashamed, had he through a silly lapse of judgement committed it or taken part in it.

The Pembroke walnut tree. (Catherine Cox)

Pembroke Old Court, where for a short while there was a walnut tree. (Jamie Collinson)

I request that the new tree be left undisturbed. No special measures will be taken to protect it, for it will be obvious to all that even the weakest of intellects could devise a means to remove it again with impunity. I hope that general opinion in the College will operate against that and that a further appeal to the good sense and conduct of individual members of the College will not be needed.
J. C. D. Hickson
TUTOR.

It was not long before the pranksters issued a notice of their own in retaliation, signing it with the college foundress' name:

The walnut tree in first court.
The tree which has again been planted in First Court was presented by three fellows to mark a long period of membership of the college and their penchant for walnuts.

It will be well known that it was twice planted last term, no doubt in good, though misplaced, humour.

It was uprooted again at the end of last term and again replanted at once. This third incident has taken the matter beyond a joke. It can now only be seen as an act of petty vandalism of which I would expect a member of the college to feel ashamed, had he through a silly lapse of judgement committed it or taken part in it.

I request that the new lawn be left undisturbed. No special measures will be taken to protect it, for it will be obvious to all that even the weakest of intellects could devise a means to replant it again with impunity. I hope that general opinion in the College will operate against that and that a further appeal to the good sense and conduct of individual members of the College will not be needed.
DE VALENCE.

PAVING THE JESUS LAWNS

A recent hoax was carried out at the end of 2009, when a (presumably Jesus College) student set out to fool his fellow students into thinking that Jesus College planned to pave over one of its famous courts. The prankster created a letter detailing the plans to cover with stone the lawns of Chapel Court. This was sure to stir up controversy within the college, as Jesus is one of the few colleges to allow students to walk on its courtyard lawns, and Chapel Court has always been a favourite for students to sit outside and revise during the exam period. Brilliantly, the letter coincided with groundwork being carried out on the lawns, and the letter contained a questionnaire about the plans, with a request to complete and return it to the college so that the voice of the student population could be heard. The letter was signed 'Siobhan Hutchins, Student Union College Liaison Officer' – neither person nor post exist – and it was not long before Ms. Hutchins' questionnaires were flooding into a confused college administration.

The use of fear, uncertainty and doubt, along with the impersonation of authority, is reminiscent of a prank/hoax I was told about by a friend's father. He had studied at the University of Manchester Institute of Science and Technology (now part of the unified University of Manchester), which was full of engineering and science students. They were no less fond of pranks than their Cambridge brethren, and during a period of minor construction work came up with a plan which blossomed into a rather successful hoax. The works being carried out were to beautify the front of the University, among other things low circular brick walls were being built, with the aim that they be filled with earth and flowers. The students noticed that the builders tended to stow their equipment overnight within these walls and hatched a plan. They snuck into the building area during the middle of the night and did a little building work of their own. Before long the walls, which were intended to be no more than a few feet high, had been built up to over 10ft. Returning the next day the builders, though they may have admired the handiwork, were not impressed at the enclosure of their equipment, and set about knocking down the walls.

This alone would have made a small but memorable prank, but the spark of genius hit, and what came next was inspired. Firstly the students telephoned the police, informing them that some students seemed to be dressed as builders and were playing some prank outside the University. As the police already had a report of the larger-than-life wall this seemed like a plausible story, and an opportunity to catch the likely culprits of the previous prank. They thanked the caller and told them they would look into it presently. Next, the students paid a visit to the builders, making sure they didn't appear too 'studenty' and told them that they'd just had a prank played on them by some students dressed as policemen, and that they should watch out for the same. The builders, by this time thoroughly fed up with students, were only too happy to take this friendly advice, and vowed to take no nonsense should anyone try it on with them. With the students returned to one of their rooms with a good view of the building work, it was not long before the police arrived. Neither side believing the other, based on their prior information, the scene quickly descended into shouting, pushing and shoving. As things heated up the students were worried they had caused a small riot, but after an agonising fifteen minutes the two sides realised they must both have been hoaxed by the same group.

This feeling of guilt, that perhaps a hoax is cruel, has gone too far, or is just simply ill conceived is often felt but rarely expressed. Clive James expressed this well in a piece for the BBC, and hit the nail on the head that for a hoax to be worthwhile it must push the boundaries of human behaviour and expose the absurd. While at Cambridge he took part in a prank which fizzled out due to simply being too mundane. As he recalled:

> I was part of a hoax once. A bunch of us from Cambridge Footlights pretended to be a team of explorers, visited a local school and

The University of Manchester prank. (Catherine Cox)

bored the sixth-formers for an entire evening with lectures about our adventures in the upper Brazilian hail forest [*sic*]. After the first half hour I started feeling queasy and had difficulty looking any of our dupes in the eye. But after an hour I could see what was really wrong with our plan. It was bound to work. There was no risk involved.

Let this be a lesson to all prospective hoaxers – if there is no risk, no mental leap for the victim to (foolishly) make, then the hoax is unlikely to be worthy of note.

ABOUT THE AUTHOR

Jamie Collinson moved to Cambridge in 2001 and graduated with a degree in mathematics from Sidney Sussex College, University of Cambridge. He fell into the world of guided punt tours and soon started his own business offering personal tours of the college backs. People often ask him why he's not working for a big bank in the City, to which he replies that he prefers messing about with boats. With all this exposure to Cambridge tomfoolery he was a natural choice to write a book about pranks, which he hopes you have enjoyed. He currently lives in Cambridge with his partner Catherine, and one day hopes to be a grown up (but not too soon).

If you're planning a visit to Cambridge, Jamie would love to take you on a tour of the river. He promises not to tell too many tall tales. You can book online at: www.cambridgerivertour.co.uk

Trinity College, Cambridge. (Linda Hall)